NEW
General Class
FCC License Preparation
Element 3B

BY
GORDON WEST
WB6NOA

FOURTH EDITION

This book was developed and published by:
Master Publishing, Inc.
Lincolnwood, Illinois

Editing by:
Pete Trotter, KB9SMG

*Thanks to Fred Maia, W5YI Group, for technical review of the RF safety
and FCC material contained in this book.*

Printing by:
Arby Graphic Service, Inc.
Lincolnwood, Illinois

Acknowledgments:
All photographs that do not have a source identification are either courtesy of
Radio Shack or Master Publishing, Inc. originals.

Fourth Edition

9   8   7   6   5   4   3   2   1

Table of Contents

QUESTION POOL NOMENCLATURE

The latest nomenclature changes and question pool numbering system recommended by the Volunteer Examiner Coordinator's Question Pool Committee (QPC) have been incorporated in this book. The General Class (Element 3B) question pool has been rewritten at the high-school reading level. This question pool is valid from July 1, 1998 until June 30, 2002.[1]

FCC RULES, REGULATIONS AND POLICIES

The NCVEC QPC releases revised question pools on a four-year cycle, and deletions as necessary. The FCC releases changes to FCC rules, regulations and policies as they are implemented. This book includes the most recent information released by the FCC at the time this copy was printed.

[1]Per QPC: "Date may be superseded as a result of changes to the licensing structure, substantial rule changes, or the like."

Preface

Welcome to your gateway for worldwide voice communications! The General Class amateur operator/primary station license allows you to operate on frequency bands to communicate worldwide both day and night. With the General Class license, you may run the maximum legal amount of power out — 1500 watts PEP. And you may operate any type of emission within the suggested band plans — telegraphy, voice, television, RTTY (radiotele-printer), and packet.

If you're a traveler with portable or hand-held equipment, the General Class license lets you stay in voice contact anywhere you go. Whether you ply the international waters of the South Seas or cruise the highways of North America, you can always stay in touch with your General Class privileges.

All of these new privileges are added to those you already enjoy in the Novice and Technician Class bands. If you hold a valid Novice, Technician, or Technician-Plus license, you may go on the air immediately after passing the General Class written examination and Morse code test that will be administered to you by a team of three volunteer examiners — fellow hams accredited by a Volunteer Examiner Coordinator (VEC).

This book covers everything you need to know to pass the General Class Element 3B written examination. You also may wish to obtain audio tapes which will help you improve your code skills and increase your CW speed to the required 13 words-per-minute (wpm). In less than a month, with just 20 minutes of study a couple of times a day, you will be adequately prepared to pass your General Class Morse practice code test. (See Chapter 2 for information on where to purchase Morse code tapes recorded by your author.)

So what are you waiting for? Start with Chapter 1 to learn about all of the General Class privileges and testing requirements. Then go on to Chapter 2, which provides helpful hints for building your code speed. Chapter 3 contains all 332 questions in the Element 3B General Class question pool that is valid from July 1, 1998 through June 30, 2002. Your volunteer examiner team will use 30 questions from this pool to make up your written examination. Chapter 4 tells you what to do before, during and after the exam. That's how easy this course is!

By the way, you'll also gain one additional privilege when you achieve General Class status. You'll be eligible to serve as a volunteer examiner to help administer Novice and Technician Class Element 2 and 3A written examinations, as well as the 5-wpm Element 1A Morse code test. Serving as a volunteer examiner is a great way to help support our Amateur Radio hobby!

We're glad you're continuing your license class advancement. I hope to hear you on the worldwide bands very soon!

Gordon West

73

Gordon West, WB6NOA

The General Class License

INTRODUCTION

The General Class amateur operator/primary station license permits you to use segments of every worldwide band for long distance voice and all other modes of amateur communications. You also keep all of the privileges you now enjoy as a Novice, Technician no-code, or Technician-Plus Class operator.

The General Class license has always been considered the "big one" because of the almost unlimited worldwide privileges this license provides you. The Novice, Technician and Technician-Plus licenses give you a taste of VHF and UHF operations, and Technician-Plus also gives you a tiny slice of the 10-meter worldwide daytime band. With the General Class license, you receive operating privileges on a segment of every worldwide band that gives you day or night skywave coverage to just about anywhere in the world.

INCENTIVE LICENSING

The General Class is the fourth in a series of six successive levels of amateur operator licenses granted by the Federal Communications Commission (FCC). Each license requires progressively higher levels of knowledge and proficiency, and each gives you additional operating privileges.

This method, known as incentive licensing, strengthens the amateur service by offering more privileges in exchange for more electronic knowledge and Morse code skill. The theory and regulations covered in each of the questions for the various examinations relate to the privileges that you will obtain as you upgrade your ham radio license. *Table 1-1* and *Table 1-2* are reminders for you of these progressive licensing examinations and code tests. *Table 1-1* gives you an overview of the classes and the examination requirements. *Table 1-2* details the subjects covered in the various written examination question elements.

CHANGES IN LICENSING BELOW GENERAL CLASS

On February 14, 1991 the Federal Communications Commission altered the entry-level path into the amateur service by creating the Technician Class license, which has no Morse code requirement. Prior to then, amateurs had to enter at the Novice Class level by passing an Element 2 written examination and an Element 1A 5-wpm Morse code test. With the creation of the Technician Class license, applicants who wish to become an amateur operator need only pass two written examinations — the 35-question Element 2 and 30-question Element 3A exams. No knowledge of Morse code is required.

Table 1-1. Amateur License Classes and Exam Requirements

License Class	Test Element	Type of Examination
Novice Class	Element 2 Element 1A	35-Question Written Examination 5-wpm code Test
[1,2] Technician Class	Elements 2 and 3A	35-Question Element 2 Written Exam 30-Question Element 3A Written Exam (No Morse code requirement)
[2] Technician-Plus Class	Element 3A Element 1A	30-Question Written Examination if a Novice 5-wpm code Test if a Technician
General Class	Element 3B Element 1B	30-Question Written Examination 13-wpm code Test
Advanced Class	Element 4A	50-Question Written Examination (No additional Morse code requirement)
Extra Class	Element 4B Element 1C	40-Question Written Examination 20-wpm code Test

[1] No-Code License
[2] Effective 2/14/91, made an official class on 6/8/94
Note: It is desirable that written examinations be taken in ascending order of difficulty all the way to Extra Class. You should not be administered Element 3B until you have passed Element 3A, etc. The code tests may be taken in *any* order. You can take the 20-wpm code test first if you can pass it. If you entered as a Technician without code, or if you entered as a Novice with code, and gained Technician-Plus by passing the Element 3A theory examination, you are eligible to apply for General Class.

Table 1-2. Question Element Subjects

Element 2
  Novice
  Technician
	Elementary theory and regulations, electronic theory, radio regulations, and RF safety

Element 3A
  Technician
  Technician-Plus
	Beginner-level amateur practices, electronic theory, radio regulations with VHF/UHF emphasis, and RF safety

Element 3B General	General operating privileges, amateur practices and radio regulations with emphasis on HF operation, and RF safety
Element 4A Advanced	Intermediate operating procedures, electronic theory, and radio regulations
Element 4B Extra	Specialized operating procedures, electronic theory, and radio regulations

Note: All license written examinations are additive. For example, to obtain a General Class license, you must take and pass an Element 2 written examination, an Element 3A written examination and an Element 3B written examination. It is better not to skip over a lower class written examination.

Individuals holding a voice-only Technician Class license can gain CW privileges by passing a 5-wpm, Element 1A Morse code test, upgrading to the Technician-Plus Class license.

Novice Class licensees, who already have demonstrated code skills, can gain Technician-Plus Class status by passing the 30-question Element 3A written examination.

PATHS TO THE GENERAL CLASS LICENSE

Here are the paths an applicant may have followed to become eligible for a General Class license.

Entry-Level — Novice Class

Amateurs who entered the service by gaining their Novice Class license passed the Element 2A written examination and the 5-wpm Element 1A Morse code test. Novice Class licensees must first pass the 30-question Element 3A written examination (gaining Technician-Plus Class) before they are eligible to take the Element 3B General Class written examination.

Entry-Level — Technician Class

Amateurs who entered the service by gaining their Technician Class license passed two written examinations — Element 2 and Element 3 A. They are eligible to take the Element 3B General Class written examination. In order to gain their General Class license, they also will be required to take and pass the 13-wpm Element 1B Morse code test, but do not need to take the Element 1A 5-wpm Morse code test required for the Novice Class license.

Entry-Level — Technician-Plus Class

Technician-Plus Class licensees have passed both the Element 2 and Element 3A written examinations, as well as the Element 1A 5-wpm Morse code test. These licensees are fully-qualified to take the General Class exam, and also will have to take and pass the 13-wpm Element 1B Morse code test.

GENERAL CLASS LICENSE REQUIREMENTS

As outlined above, you must be eligible to hold at least a Technician Class license before you are qualified to take the General Class Element 3B written examination. *You cannot skip over the Element 2 or Element 3A written examinations.* You do not need to hold the actual Technician Class license, but you must be able to demonstrate that you have passed these two examinations by having a Certificate of Successful Completion of Examination (CSCE).

You can skip over the 5-wpm Element 1A Morse code test if you can earn a passing grade on either the 13-wpm Element 1B or 20-wpm Element 1C code tests. You do not have to take the code test at the same time that you take the written examination. Once you pass the written examination, you have 365 days in which to pass the code test in order to obtain your General Class license. You also can take the code test first, and then pass the written examination within 365 days to obtain your new General Class privileges.

You are permitted to take the Element 2 and Element 3A written examinations in the same session that you take your Element 3B General Class examination. Upon successful completion of all three written examinations, as well as passing the Element 1B 13-wpm code test—all in one sitting—you will be issued a CSCE indicating your General Class status. However, you will not be able to go on the air until your actual FCC General Class license is granted—usually in about five to 15 days, depending on how your test results are filed.

"Grandfathered" Technician Class Operators

Did you take and pass the Technician Class license prior to March 21, 1987? If so, you may qualify to be "grandfathered" into the General Class.

Operators who can PROVE that their Technician Class license was issued prior to March 21, 1987—and who have not allowed their license to expire—only need to pass an Element 1B, 13-wpm or higher-speed code test to gain their General Class license. This is because the Element 3B written examination now given for the General Class license was part of the Technician Class exam prior to March 21, 1987.

Try to find a copy of your original license to check the issue date. Make sure you check for the *issue date* of your original license. Your current license probably shows the renewal date. If you cannot find your original license, you may write the Federal Communications Commission in Gettysburg, PA, and request a letter stating the original issue date of your Technician Class license and indicating your "grandfathered" status.

MORSE CODE EXEMPTIONS FOR THE HANDICAPPED

The FCC has amended its rules to make the amateur service more accessible to licensees who, because of "severe handicaps," are incapable of passing the higher-speed Morse code telegraphy examination required for General Class. However, because of international requirements, no exemptions can be granted from the 5-wpm Element 1A Morse code test.

The FCC rules require that a physician certify the handicap, and that the applicant sign a release permitting disclosure to the FCC of medical information pertinent to the handicap. The physician certification and release form are located on the back of the Form 610 license application. If you believe you qualify for an exemption, have your physician read and sign the certification. You also should know that the FCC has ruled that the term "physician" is limited only to doctors of medicine (MDs) and doctors of osteopathy (DOs).

ELEMENT 3B EXAMINATION CONTENT

Table 1-3 shows how the 30 questions on your General Class written examination are derived from the full Element 3B question pool, which contains a total of 332 questions used to make up your exam. Subelement G0, on RF safety, has been added effective July 1, 1998. This adds five questions on RF safety to the written exam. This new edition of *General Class* contains the current question pool—including the subelement on RF safety—that is in effect from July 1, 1998 through June 30, 2002.

Table 1-3. Question Distribution for the General Class Exam

Subelement		Number of Questions
G1	Commission's Rules	4
	(FCC rules for the amateur radio services)	
G2	Operating Procedures	3
	(Amateur station operating procedures)	
G3	Radio Wave Propagation	3
	(Radio wave propagation characteristics of amateur service frequency bands)	
G4	Amateur Radio Practices	5
	(Amateur radio practices)	
G5	Electrical Principles	2
	(Electrical principles as applied to amateur station equipment)	
G6	Circuit Components	1
	(Amateur station equipment circuit components)	
G7	Practical Circuits	1
	(Practical circuits employed in amateur station equipment)	
G8	Signals and Emissions	2
	(Signals and emissions transmitted by amateur stations)	
G9	Antennas and Feed Lines	4
	(Amateur station antennas and feed lines)	
G0	RF Safety	5
	(Radiofrequency environmental safety practices at an amateur station)	
	TOTAL	30

Titles in parenthesis are the official subelement titles listed in FCC Part 97.

GENERAL CLASS LICENSE PRIVILEGES

Figure 1-1 graphically illustrates your new General Class code and voice privileges on the medium-frequency (MF) bands (300 kHz-3 MHz) and high-frequency (HF) bands (3 MHz-30 MHz). Code privileges are in the designated area on the left side of each band, and voice privileges are in the designated area on the right side of each band. Designated areas between the code and voice privileges have no privileges for the General Class; these are reserved for Advanced and Extra Class operators.

As you can see, Advanced and Extra Class operators have the same *band* privileges that you will have as a General Class operator, they just have a little bit more elbow room. But don't worry—there is plenty of room throughout the General Class voice spectrum for working the world!

160 Meters, 1.8 MHz-2.0 MHz

Your General Class privileges are the same as Advanced and Extra on this band. You may operate voice and code from one end to the other. The 160-meter band is great for long-distance, nighttime communications. It's located just above the AM broadcast radio frequencies. At night, 160 meters lets you work the world.

80 Meters, 3.5 MHz-4.0 MHz

General Class code, data, and radioteleprinter (RTTY) privileges are from 3525 kHz to 3750 kHz. Single-sideband voice privileges are from 3850 kHz to 4000 kHz. During the day, range is limited to about 400 miles. However, at night, you can work well over 3000 miles away! Novice CW privileges have been shifted to 3675-3725 kHz.

40 Meters, 7 MHz-7.3 MHz

On this band, General Class code, data, and RTTY privileges are from 7025 kHz to 7150 kHz. Single-sideband voice for General Class is allowed from 7225 kHz to 7300 kHz. During daylight hours, 40 meters is great for base and mobile contacts up to 500 miles away. At night, 40 meters is a wonderful band for worldwide DXing. However, 40 meters also is shared with worldwide AM shortwave broadcast stations so, at night, be prepared to dodge megawatt carriers playing everything from rock-and-roll to political broadcasts.

30 Meters, 10.1 MHz-10.15 MHz

Only code, data, and RTTY are permitted on this band. Thirty meters is located just above the 10-MHz WWV time broadcasts on shortwave radio. Voice is not allowed on this band by any class of amateur operator, and power is limited to 200 watts PEP.

20 Meters, 14 MHz-14.350 MHz

This is the best DX worldwide band there is, day or night! Morse code, data, and radioteleprinter (RTTY) privileges extend from 14.025 MHz to 14.150 MHz. General Class voice privileges extend from 14.225 MHz to 14.350 MHz. This is where the real DX activity takes place. Almost 24 hours a day, you should be able to work stations in excess of 5000 miles away with a modest antenna setup on the 20-meter band. If you are a mariner, most of the long range maritime mobile bands are within your privileges as a General Class operator. If you are into recreational vehicles (RV's), there are nets all over the country especially for you. The band "where it's at" is 20 meters when you want to work the world from your car, boat, RV, or home shack!

17 Meters, 18.068 MHz-18.168 MHz

There is plenty of elbow room here with lots of foreign DX coming in day and night. Most new base antennas have 17 meters included. All emission types are authorized on this newer Amateur Radio band.

15 Meters, 21 MHz-21.450 MHz

General Class CW, data, and RTTY privileges extend from 21.025 to 21.200 MHz. Your single-sideband voice privileges are from 21.3 to 21.450 MHz. The 15-meter band is loved by hams throughout the world because it has extremely low noise. There is little power line noise on 15 meters, and there is almost no static. Band conditions on 15 meters usually favor daytime and evening contacts in the direction of the sun. Late at night, 15 meters begins to fade and you won't get skywave coverage until the next morning. However, when signals come in strong on 15 meters, they just about pin your S-meter. Fifteen meters is a popular band for mobile operators because antenna requirements are small. Because of the very low noise on 15 meters, you can

WORLDWIDE SPECTRUM

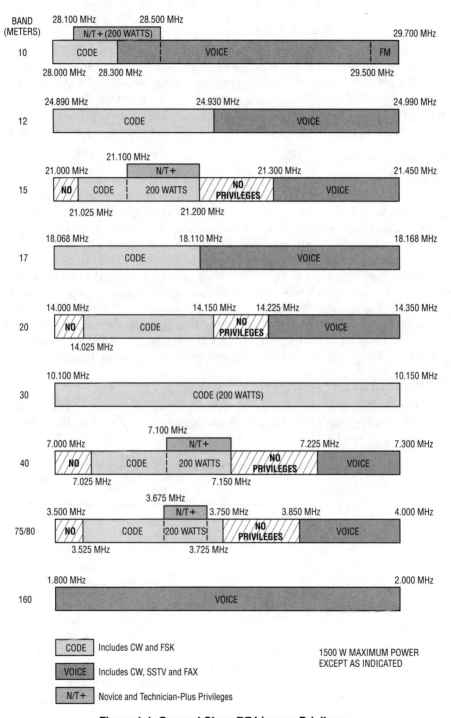

Figure 1-1. General Class RF License Privileges

work the world easily with just 10 watts of power (although, as a General Class operator, you are allowed up to 1500 watts of power output).

12 Meters, 24.890 MHz-24.990 MHz

Code, data, and RTTY privileges on the 12-meter band extend from 24.890 MHz to 24.930 MHz. Voice privileges are from 24.930 to 24.990 MHz. You have the same privileges and elbow room as the Advanced and Extra Class operator, too. Although this is a very narrow band, expect excellent daytime range throughout the world. At night, range is limited to groundwave coverage because the ionosphere is not receiving sunlight to produce skywave coverage.

10 Meters, 28 MHz-29.7 MHz

General Class CW, data, and RTTY privileges begin at the very bottom of the band, 28.0 MHz, and extend up to 28.3 MHz. Your voice privileges begin immediately at 28.3 MHz and extend to 29.7 MHz. You have the same privileges as the Advanced and Extra Class operator on 10 meters. You should already know about 10 meters since Novice and Technician-Plus Class operators can operate on 10 meters using code from 28.1 MHz to 28.3 MHz and voice from 28.3 MHz to 28.5 MHz. Now you get to roam the entire band with your General Class license! Most of the activity is usually found down in the Novice/Technician-Plus Class portion of the band, 28.3 MHz to 28.5 MHz. You might even try your hand at operating frequency modulation (FM), which is permitted above 29.5 MHz. Listen for FM simplex activity at 29.6 MHz; you'll even find some 10-meter FM repeaters at the top of the band, too.

6 Meters and Up

Your General Class license allows you unlimited band privileges and unlimited emission privileges on several higher-frequency bands, as shown in *Table 1-4*.

Table 1-4. 6 Meter and Higher Band Privileges

Frequency	Meters
50–54 MHz	6 meters
144–148 MHz	2 meters
222–225 MHz	1.25 meters
420–450 MHz	.70 meters (70 cm)
902–928 MHz	.35 meters (35 cm)
1240–1300 MHz	.23 meters (23 cm)

Microwave Bands

Your General Class license allows you unlimited band privileges and unlimited emission privileges in the microwave bands, as indicated in *Table 1-5*. These VHF, UHF, and SHF frequencies are the same ones for which you received privileges when you passed your Technician or Technician-Plus Class examinations.

Table 1-5. Microwave Band Frequency Privileges

Frequency	Frequency
2300–2310 MHz	47.0–47.2 GHz
2390–2450 MHz	75.5–81.0 GHz
3.3–3.5 GHz	119.98–120.02 GHz
5.65–5.925 GHz	142–149 GHz
10.0–10.5 GHz	241–250 GHz
24.0–24.25 GHz	All above 300 GHz

For a detailed explanation of these VHF and UHF bands, refer to *Technician No-Code Plus* for Novice and Technician Classes, authored by Gordon West, and available from Radio Shack (RS# 62-2426) stores, local Amateur Radio dealers, or by calling W5YI Group at 800/669-9594. This book examines the VHF, UHF and SHF bands in detail, and presents the specific ARRL-recommended band plans.

Novice, Technician, and Technician-Plus Class Exam Administration

There is one more very important privilege you gain when you achieve General Class status. As a General Class licensee, you may take part in the administration of Novice and Technician Class examinations. Once you are accredited by a local or national volunteer-examiner coordinator, you can join a three-member team to give these tests.

The volunteer examination system specifically allows three Generals to form an accredited team to give the Novice and Technician Class examinations, including the 5-wpm code test, to anyone wishing to get started in the fabulous ham radio hobby.

So, if you wish to see the amateur service grow in your local area, find two other General Class operators, contact a local or national VEC for accreditation, and start your own testing team for beginners.

SUMMARY

So there you have it—a look at some of the exciting privileges awaiting you with a General Class license. Undoubtedly the biggest privilege is gaining voice access to every worldwide band allocated to the amateur service. These new worldwide band privileges, coupled with all modes of operation, plus 1500 watts of power output, will certainly give you some DX excitement as you talk to the world. (Note: General Class operators are limited to 200 watts PEP transmitter power between 3.675-3.725 MHz, 7.10-7.15 MHz, 10.10-10.15 MHz, and 21.1-21.2 MHz.)

Are you ready to prepare for the written General class examination? Even though your test has grown from 25 to 30 multiple-choice questions, the 5 additional questions on RF safety are easy to understand and important for you to know when you start bringing in all that new equipment and big antennas to communicate throughout the world on high frequency.

2

Building CW Speed to 13 WPM

GENERAL CLASS MORSE CODE TEST REQUIREMENTS

The speed requirement for the Element 1B Morse code test for the General Class operator's license is 13 words-per-minute (wpm). This requirement is about in the middle of what other nations require of ham operators for their amateur service worldwide privileges. France, for example, has only a 10-wpm requirement, while Napal requires candidates to pass a 29-wpm Morse code test in order to gain worldwide privileges. So, the United States' 13-wpm General Class code requirement is one of the easiest CW tests to pass. You can do it!

ABOUT THE TEST

First, we'll look at the requirements for the test. Then we'll discuss some study methods to help you improve your Morse code speed to 13 wpm.

Test Administration

The Element 1B Morse code test is administered by a team of three volunteer examiners (VEs) who are accredited by a VEC. These VEs may make up their own code test, or use one supplied on cassette tape or computer disk from a VEC. Regardless of who makes up the code test, the CW portion of your General Class examination is fairly well standardized throughout the country.

Test Speed

An FCC Notice dated June 22, 1982, recommended that the Element 1B 13-wpm code test be generated at a 15-wpm character speed with spaces in between the characters to slow the rate to 13-wpm. This is "regular Farnsworth" spacing. This means that you won't hear a code test recorded at a 25-wpm rate with big spaces to slow the message to 13-wpm. So the code test you will listen to will be relatively slow and distinct.

The American Radio Relay League (ARRL) generates its code tests for General Class at an 18-wpm character rate (known as "fast Farnsworth") spaced out to the 13-wpm rate. The ARRL examinations are characterized by slightly shorter and more compact dits and dahs, with longer spaces between each character. You can hear this "fast Farnsworth" rate over the air by tuning to the ARRL code practice frequencies listed on page 14.

Test Message and Questions

Your General Class code test message will last a minimum of 5 minutes, preceded by a 1-minute warm-up that lets you adjust to the acoustics of the room. Some VEs provide headphones, while others use a professional tape player and speaker system to reproduce the code message.

The 5-minute code test at 13-wpm most likely will be a "QSO" type of message. It will be as if you tuned into one amateur operator communicating with another. Your challenge is to copy the message as best you can. VEs usually allow ample time after the test message ends for you to correct your code copy. You usually are not required to send any code for the test, just receive.

There are two ways to pass the text. The first is by copying one full minute of perfect copy that agrees with the test message. This means correctly copying 65 characters in a row. Punctuation, numerals, and prosigns count as two characters. When you turn in your telegraphy copy sheet, the VEs will check your copy to see if you accomplished this.

The second way to pass the test is by answering a 10-question written quiz about the test message. This is usually a "fill in the blank" or "multiple choice" test. If you answer 7 out of 10 questions correctly, you pass.

Typical Message

Here is a sample 13-wpm QSO that could be used on a General Class code test:

Warmup

THIS IS A 1 MINUTE WARMUP FOR THE ADJUSTMENT OF THE TAPE PLAYER. GOOD LUCK.

Actual Exam Message

After the warm-up message, a spoken announcement tells you that the test is about to begin.

VVV VVV N6RUZ DE K4SUN RRR TNX SAM FOR THE CALL. UR RST 559 $\overline{\text{BT}}$ 559. NAME HERE IS WILBUR. QTH IS MIAMI, FLORIDA. MY RIG IS A COLLINS KWM2 AND RUNS 75 WATTS INTO A WIRE LOOP UP JUST 10 FEET. THE WEATHER IS HOT/SUNNY, AND TEMPERATURE IS 88 DEGREES. AGE IS 93, AND LICENSE IS A NOVICE. OCCUPATION IS RETIRED DOCTOR. I MUST QRT FOR A CAT NAP. HOW COPY? N6RUZ DE K4SUN $\overline{\text{AR}}$ $\overline{\text{SK}}$.

The General Class code test usually begins with a series of six Vs, then goes right into call signs. Call signs are sometimes hard to copy but, since they are often repeated at the end, you have two chances to copy them. Try exceptionally hard to get those call letters. Seldom does an examiner put in misspellings or deceptive QSOs (such as a weather report of 100 degrees in Alaska).

If you look carefully at the message, you will find that it contains all letters of the alphabet, numerals 0-9, period, comma, question mark, slant bar

($\overline{\text{DN}}$), the break or pause ($\overline{\text{BT}}$), and sign-off signals $\overline{\text{AR}}$ and $\overline{\text{SK}}$. The requirement to include all of these is spelled out in FCC Section 97.503(a).

Typical Questions

The following are typical questions your VE Team (VET) would ask after you
have copied the coded QSO message:

1. What was the call sign of the sending operator? (K4SUN)
2. What was the name of the sending operator? (Wilbur)
3. What was the RST report given? (559 $\overline{\text{BT}}$ 559)
4. What was the QTH of the sending operator? (Miami, Florida)
5. What type of transceiver was the sending operator using? (Collins KWM2)
6. What type of antenna was the sending operator using? (Wire Loop)
7. What was the power output in watts of the sending operator's rig? (75 watts)
8. What were the weather conditions at the sending operator's location? (Hot/Sunny)
9. What was the occupation of the sending operator? (Retired Doctor)
10. Why did the sending operator go QRT? (Cat Nap)

After Copying the Code

Even if you didn't copy the code 100 percent, letter-for-letter, you should still
be able to extract enough information to correctly answer 10 questions similar
to those above. If the answers are multiple-choice, all the better!

If you determine that you did just great for about one minute during the
middle of the message, but goofed up at the beginning and end, you may want
to try for the one minute of solid copy. You will usually have time after the
examination to correct your copy, regardless of what type of message is sent.

Second Chance

It is not at all uncommon to "freeze up" during the actual code test. If you
should flunk the test the first time through, ask your examination team if
they will allow you to take another code test a few minutes later. If so, they
will require you to pay a second test fee, and, of course, the second test message will be different from the first one. Many times a person passing that
big 13-wpm code test is successful on the second try.

PRACTICING FOR THE CODE TEST

There are three recommended ways for you to practice your Morse code skills
and build your speed to the required 13-wpm. First, use audio tapes recorded
to help amateur operators practice their skills. Second, use a computer
program to generate practice tests and to practice those hard letters. Third,
listen to other sources of code, such as the ARRL broadcasts, to get used to
how other code sounds, not just the practice tapes.

Code Tapes

Code tapes to help you learn the Morse code and build your speed have been recorded by your author, Gordon West, and are available from Radio Shack and other sources. *Learning Morse Code* (Radio Shack #62-2418) is a set of four tapes designed to teach you the code for the 5-wpm Novice Class test, and the 13-wpm General Class test. These tapes are recorded at 15- and 18-wpm character rates, with spaces added between the characters to slow the message to the 5-wpm and 13-wpm rate. This gives you a little edge because you are over-preparing for the actual test.

A more comprehensive set of Morse code tapes, *Gordon West Ultimate Code Tapes*, are available from the W5YI Group (order by calling 1-800-669-9594). There are three courses, one for Novice Class (5-wpm), one for General Class (13-wpm), and one for Extra Class (20-wpm). Each course contains six tapes designed to help you learn the code, build your speed, and pass that test!

You will find the code-training tapes fun listening and humorous, as well as educational. You may think you're beginning to memorize words and phrases on the test preparation tapes, and that's what we want you to do! You will find yourself memorizing common words found in most ham radio communications. And you'll learn how to anticipate where certain characters may be used. For example, you will find that the slant bar ($\overline{\text{DN}}$) usually is used between the weather reports (cold/windy). The pause, or break ($\overline{\text{BT}}$), may be used between RST reports (589 $\overline{\text{BT}}$ 589).

How to Use the Tapes

The code cassette speed-building tapes are fully narrated and may be played almost anywhere. The best practice is to write down the code, rather than just listening and memorizing it. Always practice copying the code to paper.

Copy for 20-Minute Segments: Start a notebook at 5 wpm, and keep track of your progress listening to these cassette tapes. Play the code tapes for only about 20 minutes, and then take a break for several hours. It's far better to study for 20 minutes three times a day, than it is to go for a 1-1/2 hour marathon brain-out.

Listen Carefully: Listen carefully to the instructions on the code cassettes. Every lesson is under 20 minutes, and this makes for perfect practice two or three times a day.

Try to Go Faster: Continually push yourself to go on to a faster rate on the code tapes. Once you have mastered a code segment so you can copy 75 percent correctly, push on. Don't try to get 100 percent perfect copy—few ham radio operators copy code perfectly.

Don't Read As You Copy: Don't try to read the message as you are copying it—put your hand over it, and keep your eyes on your pen or pencil as you write the next letter. Don't anticipate or try to second guess what's coming next! After the code test is over, you will have plenty of time to go back and correct your copy.

Missing Characters: If you miss a letter or number, put a little "peck" mark on your paper and catch the very next letter. Chances are you can easily figure out the missing letter later by looking at the entire word. However, if you try to determine that letter during the actual code test, chances are you're going to miss the next few letters, or maybe words. Copy letter for letter, and don't let a missed letter throw you!

MORSE CODE COMPUTER PROGRAMS

Another great way to learn the code and practice for your General, and even your Extra Class code tests, is with computer software. Practice just on those tough letters, or let the computer create a sample code test for you. The popularity of portable laptop computers makes code learning fun on the keyboard.

Table 2-1. Radio Frequencies for Code Reception

Pacific	Mtn	Cent	East	Sun	Mon	Tue	Wed	Thu	Fri	Sat
6 am	7 am	8 am	9 am					Fast Code	Slow Code	
7 am	8 am	9 am	10am					Code Bulletin		
8 am	9 am	10 am	11 am					Teleprinter Bulletin		
9 am	10 am	11 am	noon							
10 am	11 am	noon	1 pm							
11 am	noon	1 pm	2 pm		**VISITING OPERATOR TIME**					
noon	1 pm	2 pm	3 pm							
1 pm	2 pm	3 pm	4 pm	Slow Code	Fast Code	Slow Code	Fast Code	Slow Code	Fast Code	Slow Code
2 pm	3 pm	4 pm	5 pm			Code Bulletin				
3 pm	4 pm	5 pm	6 pm			Teleprinter Bulletin				
4 pm	5 pm	6 pm	7 pm	Fast Code	Slow Code	Fast Code	Slow Code	Fast Code	Slow Code	Fast Code
5 pm	6 pm	7 pm	8 pm			Code Bulletin				
6 pm	7 pm	8 pm	9 pm			Teleprinter Bulletin				
6^{45} pm	7^{45} pm	8^{45} pm	9^{45} pm			Voice Bulletin				
7 pm	8 pm	9 pm	10 pm	Slow Code	Fast Code	Slow Code	Fast Code	Slow Code	Fast Code	Slow Code
8 pm	9 pm	10 pm	11 pm			Code Bulletin				
9 pm	10 pm	11 pm	Mdnte			Teleprinter Bulletin				
9^{45} pm	10^{45} pm	11^{45} pm	12^{45} am			Voice Bulletin				

☐ **Morse code transmissions:**

Frequencies are 1.818, 3.5815, 7.0475, 14.0475, 18.0975, 21.0675, 28.0675 and 147.555 MHz.

Slow Code = practice sent at 5, 71/2, 10, 13 and 15 wpm.

Fast Code = practice sent at 35, 30, 25, 20, 15, 13 and 10 wpm.

Code practice text is from the pages of *QST*. The source is given at the beginning of each practice session and alternate speeds within each session. For example, "Text is from July 1992 QST, pages 9 and 81," indicates that the plain text is from the article on page 9 and mixed number/letter groups are from page 81.

Code bulletins are sent at 18 wpm. Source: *QST Magazine*

LISTEN TO OTHER SOURCES

For the code tapes to be effective, we recommend you listen to Morse code from other sources as well. *Table 2-1* lists many frequencies where you can copy CW sent between 5 wpm and 15 wpm. On-the-air code practice is an excellent way to increase code speed. If you have a high-frequency transceiver with a Novice license or Technician-Plus Class privileges, you have four worldwide bands that you can go on the air using Morse code right now. Don't miss this valuable opportunity to increase your code proficiency.

Practice, Practice, Practice

Listen to any type of code that you think you have a chance of copying. Don't worry about code that doesn't sound exactly like the test preparation tapes— any code will do. With almost any type of shortwave radio receiver, you can pick up hundreds of code broadcasts. Also, there are many code cassettes on the market; and as long as you can make out the dits and dahs, it's good practice.

WHEN TO TAKE THE TEST

The General Class code test, Element 1B, may be taken anytime you feel ready. In fact, you may take a code test for Extra, General, or Novice anytime regardless of your advancement through the written examinations. However, you can't go on the air as a General Class operator until you have passed the General Class written examination and its prerequisites (Element 2 and 3A) plus the 13-wpm code test (Element 1B).

If you wake up one morning and feel very confident that you can pass the code test, take it. If you pass the test, you receive a one-year certificate for the code completion; that gives you 365 days to pass the written examination and complete the total requirements. If you have code experience and have sharpened your skills, you might want to go ahead and take the 20-wpm code test, which is required for the Extra Class license. Passing it would give you two steps in one (General and Extra) because it also gives you complete credit for the General 13-wpm test. If you did go ahead and pass the 20-wpm code test, satisfying the code portion of your Extra Class operator's license, you would have 365 days to complete the Advanced and Extra Class written examinations.

Don't let the code requirement stand in the way of your General Class upgrade. Study the code, listen to the tapes and CW broadcasts, and you can pass that 13-wpm Morse code test!

3

Getting Ready for the Written Examination

ABOUT THIS CHAPTER

This chapter covers all the possible, exact questions and answers from the 332-question Element 3B question pool that will be used to make up your 30-question General Class written examination. Your examination will be divided into ten subelements, as shown in *Table 3-1*. Each subelement has a specific number of possible questions and a specific number of actual questions that will be on the written examination. Carefully study *Table 3-1* so you will understand how the possible and actual questions are distributed among the ten subelements.

Table 3-1. Question Pool

Subelement		Page	Total Questions	Examination Questions
G1	Commission's Rules	20	46	4
G2	Operating Procedures	32	33	3
G3	Radio Wave Propagation	41	33	3
G4	Amateur Radio Practices	50	55	5
G5	Electrical Principles	67	22	2
G6	Circuit Components	74	11	1
G7	Practical Circuits	77	11	1
G8	Signals and Emissions	79	22	2
G9	Antennas and Feed Lines	85	44	4
G0	RF Safety	97	55	5
TOTAL			332	30

Your examination will have exactly 30 questions with 4 multiple-choice answers per question. You must answer 74 percent of the questions correctly, which means that you must answer 22 questions correctly.

Your 30 questions will be selected word-for-word from the 332 question pool contained in this chapter. Each question has four possible multiple-choice answers. The correct answer to each question is given along with a discussion on why it is indeed the right one.

WHAT THE EXAM CONTAINS

The examination questions of all license class levels and their appropriate multiple-choice answers are public information. FCC rules prohibit any examiner or examination team from making any changes to any questions, including any numerical values! No numbers, words, letters, or punctuation marks may be altered from the published question pool. Thus, the questions in this book are exactly as they will appear on your examination. In addition, the same four multiple-choice answers must be worded on the test exactly as they are published here. However, their A, B, C, D order may be changed.

All amateur operator examination questions are reviewed every four years by a team of volunteer-examiner coordinators (VECs). These are fellow hams with Extra Class licenses who volunteer their time to ensure today's tests are accurate and fair, and the subject matter relevant. As technology changes, so will the questions. A public notice will be given one year in advance for any question changes so book publishers can revise their study materials.

NEW JULY 1, 1998, GENERAL CLASS QUESTION POOL

This edition of *General Class* has been revised to include the new Element 3B General Class question pool that is in effect from July 1, 1998 through June 30, 2002. The question pool was developed by the Volunteer Examiner Coordinator (VEC) Question Pool Committee (QPC) under the leadership of committee chairman Ray Adams, W4CPA. A special thank you goes to Steve Sternitzke, NS5I, for his efforts compiling the many drafts of the question pool, and to Fred Maia, W5YI, for his contributions to the new Subelement 0 on RF safety.

The QPC welcomes comments from the amateur radio community, and many such suggestions have been incorporated into this new question pool. Comments may be sent to: Question Pool Committee, Ray Adams, W4CPA, Chairman, 5833 Clinton Hwy., Suite 203, Knoxville, TN 37912-2500.

Question Coding

Each question of the 332 General Class question pool has a number and letter coding system assigned to it. *Figure 3-1* explains the coding for question G8B01.

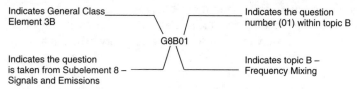

Figure 3-1. Examination Question Coding

The coded numbers and letters reveal important facts about each question. Each subelement has a topic number within it. Each topic has a letter, and the question within each topic has a two-digit number beginning with 01. Therefore, G8B01 indicates the question is an Element 3B General Class question from Subelement 8, Signals and Emissions. It is the first (01) question from topic B, Frequency Mixing, Multiplication, Bandwidths, and HF Data Communications.

You probably are saying, "332 questions sounds like an impossible memory job." GOOD NEWS—almost every question is asked at least twice with some slightly different phraseology. This means you only have to memorize about 166 questions asked a couple of different ways. You can do that easily, right?

Examination Questions

FCC Rule 97.523 requires each question pool to contain at least 10 times the number of questions that are to be on any examination taken from that pool. Although this "10 times" rule applies only to the entire question pool, the Question Pool Committee has applied it to each subelement and each subelement topic. This makes it easier for you to figure out exactly where the questions will be taken from for your upcoming examination. You should never have more than one question taken from each topic.

HINTS ON STUDYING FOR THE EXAM

All of the material that you need to study for your General Class examination is in this chapter, organized in a convenient format. Here are some suggestions to make your learning easier:

1. Begin with the first subelement, G1A. Study the question, the correct answer, and the brief explanation to better understand the importance of the question and why the answer is correct. It's also a good idea to look at the incorrect answers for some additional pointers on why the correct answer is indeed the right one.
2. Be sure to read over each multiple-choice answer carefully. Some start out looking good, but just one or two words may change the answer from right to wrong. Also, don't anticipate that the multiple-choice answers will always appear in exactly the same A, B, C, D order on your General Class exam; *some examiners may change the order*.
3. Keep in mind how many questions may be taken from any one topic. For instance, although there are 11 total questions in Subelement G7A, Practical Circuits, only one question will be selected for your upcoming exam out of the 11 questions from this entire subelement.
4. A fun way of preparing for the exam is to let someone else read the correct answer, and you try to recite the exact General Class question!
5. Once you have memorized most of the questions and correct answers, put a check mark beside those you know forward and backward. Then concentrate on the remaining harder questions that may require better understanding and more memorization. Put a check mark beside them as you memorize them.
6. Try a practice written exam and see how well you do. Ask a friend to give you a sample test by picking a series of questions according to the distribution shown in *Table 3-1*.
7. On those particularly hard questions, make up flash cards with the question on one side and the four possible answers on the reverse side. See if you can pick out the right answer.

WRITTEN EXAMINATION QUESTION POOL

So here you go—332 questions, many almost duplicates of others but changed in wording, for your General Class written exam preparation. The syllabus used for the development of the question pool is included as an aid in studying the subelements and topic groups. Review the syllabus before you start your study to gain an understanding of the question pool details.

Element 3B (General Class) Syllabus

G1 – Commission's Rules
(4 exam questions – 4 groups)
G1A General control operator frequency privileges; local control; repeater and harmful interference definitions; third-party communication

G1B Antenna structure limitations; good engineering and good amateur practice; beacon operation; restricted operation; retransmitting radio signals

G1C Transmitter power standards; type acceptance of external RF power amplifiers; standards for type acceptance of external RF power amplifiers; HF data emission standards

G1D Examination element preparation; examination administration; temporary station identification

G2 – Operating Procedures
(3 exam questions – 3 groups)
G2A Phone; RTTY; repeater; VOX and full break-in CW

G2B Operating courtesy; antenna orientation and HF operations, including logging practices; ITU regions

G2C Emergencies, including drills; communications and amateur auxiliary to the FCC's Compliance and Information Bureau

G3 – Radio Wave Propagation
(3 exam questions – 3 groups)
G3A Ionospheric disturbances; sunspots and solar radiation

G3B Maximum usable frequency; propagation "hops"

G3C Height of ionospheric regions; critical angle and frequency; HF scatter

G4 – Amateur Radio Practices
(5 exam questions – 5 groups)
G4A Two-tone test; electronic TR switch; amplifier neutralization

G4B Test equipment: oscilloscope; signal tracer; antenna noise bridge; monitoring oscilloscope; field-strength meters

G4C Audio rectification in consumer electronics; RF ground

G4D Speech processors; PEP calculations; wire sizes and fuses

G4E Common connectors used in amateur stations; types; when to use; fastening methods; precautions when using; HF mobile radio installations; emergency power systems; generators; battery storage devices and charging sources, including solar; wind generation

G5 – Electrical Principles
(2 exam questions – 2 groups)
G5A Impedance, including matching; resistance, including ohm; reactance, inductance, capacitance and metric divisions of these values

G5B Decibel; Ohm's law; current and voltage dividers; electrical power calculations and series and parallel components; transformers (either voltage or impedance); sine wave root-mean-square (RMS) value

G6 – Circuit Components
(1 exam question – 1 group)
G6A Resistors; capacitors; inductors; rectifiers; and transistors; etc.

G7 – Practical Circuits
(1 exam question – 1 group)
G7A Power supplies and filters; single-sideband transmitters and receivers

G8 – Signals and Emissions
(2 exam questions – 2 groups)
G8A Signal information; AM; FM; single and double sideband and carrier; bandwidth; modulation envelope; deviation; overmodulation

G8B Frequency mixing; multiplication; bandwidths; HF data communications

G9 – Antennas and Feed Lines
(4 exam questions – 4 groups)
G9A Yagi antennas – physical dimensions; impedance matching; radiation patterns; directivity and major lobes

G9B Loop antennas – physical dimensions; impedance matching; radiation patterns; directivity and major lobes

G9C Random wire antennas – physical dimensions; impedance matching; radiation patterns; directivity and major lobes; feedpoint impedance of 1/2-wavelength dipole and 1/4-wavelength vertical antennas

G9D Popular antenna feed-lines – characteristic impedance and impedance matching; SWR calculations

G0 – RF Safety
(5 exam questions – 5 groups)
G0A Safety principles
G0B RF safety rules and guidelines
G0C Routine station evaluation and measurements
G0D Practical RF safety applications
G0E RF safety solutions

Subelement G1 – Commission's Rules

(4 exam questions – 4 topic groups)

Note: A Part § 97 reference is enclosed in brackets, e.g., [97], after each correct answer explanation in this subelement.

G1A General control operator frequency privileges; local control; repeater and harmful interference definitions; third-party communications

G1A01 What are the frequency limits for General class operators in the 160-meter band (ITU Region 2)?
A. 1800 - 1900-kHz
B. 1900 - 2000-kHz
C. 1800 - 2000-kHz
D. 1825 - 2000-kHz

ANSWER C: The 160-meter wavelength band privileges are shown for General Class licensees. When you pass the upcoming General examination, you will have access to this entire band. 160 meters is a fun band for nighttime contacts. [97.301d]

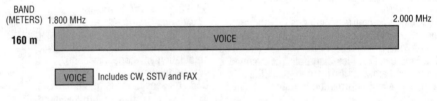

160-Meter Wavelength Band Privileges

G1A02 What are the frequency limits for General class operators in the 75/80-meter band (ITU Region 2)?
A. 3525 - 3750-kHz and 3850 - 4000-kHz
B. 3525 - 3775-kHz and 3875 - 4000-kHz
C. 3525 - 3750-kHz and 3875 - 4000-kHz
D. 3525 - 3775-kHz and 3850 - 4000-kHz

ANSWER A: General Class CW privileges begin at 3525 kHz, 25 kHz above the band edge, and go to 3750 kHz. Your new voice privileges then start at 3850 kHz and go to the top of the band—4000 kHz. The frequencies in between the CW and voice portions of this band are reserved for higher-class operators. The correct answer has two "50's." [97.301d]

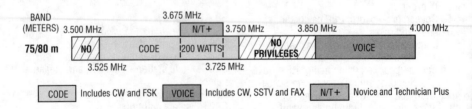

75/80-Meter Wavelength Band Privileges

G1A03 What are the frequency limits for General class operators in the 40-meter band (ITU Region 2)?

A. 7025 - 7175-kHz and 7200 - 7300-kHz
B. 7025 - 7175-kHz and 7225 - 7300-kHz
C. 7025 - 7150-kHz and 7200 - 7300-kHz
D. 7025 - 7150-kHz and 7225 - 7300-kHz

ANSWER D: Your new General Class CW privileges begin 25 kHz above the bottom of the band edge. 7025 kHz to 7150 kHz is great for daytime and nighttime CW. From 7150 kHz to 7225 kHz, you have no privileges. 7225 kHz to 7300 kHz is where all the voice action is on 40 meters. Spot the correct answer as 25-50-25. [97.301d]

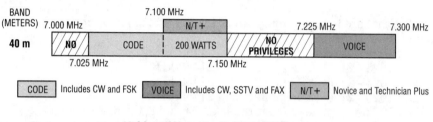

40-Meter Wavelength Band Privileges

G1A04 What are the frequency limits for General class operators in the 30-meter band?

A. 10100 - 10150-kHz
B. 10100 - 10175-kHz
C. 10125 - 10150-kHz
D. 10125 - 10175-kHz

ANSWER A: As a new General Class operator, you get the entire 30-meter band from 10.1 MHz to 10.15 MHz. This is a CW/DATA/FSK band only—no voice. [97.301d]

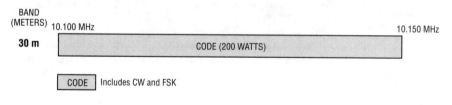

30-Meter Wavelength Band Privileges

G1A05 What are the frequency limits for General class operators in the 20-meter band?

A. 14025 - 14100-kHz and 14175 - 14350-kHz
B. 14025 - 14150-kHz and 14225 - 14350-kHz
C. 14025 - 14125-kHz and 14200 - 14350-kHz
D. 14025 - 14175-kHz and 14250 - 14350-kHz

ANSWER B: The 20-meter wavelength band is the most popular band in the world for day and night long-range DX. Your code privileges begin 25 kHz above the bottom band edge, and extend up to 14.15 MHz. Your voice privileges start at 14.225 MHz, up to the top of the band at 14.350 MHz. Spot the correct answer as 25-50-25. [97.301d]

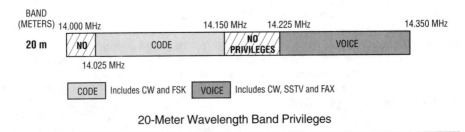

20-Meter Wavelength Band Privileges

G1A06 What are the frequency limits for General class operators in the 15-meter band?
   A. 21025 - 21200-kHz and 21275 - 21450-kHz
   B. 21025 - 21150-kHz and 21300 - 21450-kHz
   C. 21025 - 21150-kHz and 21275 - 21450-kHz
   D. 21025 - 21200-kHz and 21300 - 21450-kHz

ANSWER D: The 15-meter band is great for DX during the day and evening hours. Your General Class CW privileges begin 25 kHz above the bottom band edge, and extend to 21.2 MHz. Your voice privileges start at 21.3 MHz, and go to the top of the band to 21.45 MHz. Spot the correct answer by remembering that you have no privileges between 21200 MHz to 21300 MHz. These frequencies are reserved for higher-class licensees. [97.301d]

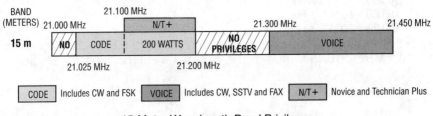

15-Meter Wavelength Band Privileges

G1A07 What are the frequency limits for General class operators in the 12-meter band?
   A. 24890 - 24990-kHz
   B. 24890 - 24975-kHz
   C. 24900 - 24990-kHz
   D. 24900 - 24975-kHz

ANSWER A: You get the entire 12-meter band as a General Class operator—from top to bottom—24.890 to 24.990 MHz. There is very little activity on this band, so have fun working some great daytime DX. [97.301d]

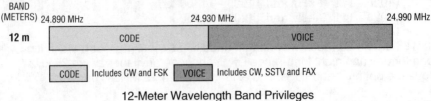

12-Meter Wavelength Band Privileges

G1A08 What are the frequency limits for General class operators in the 10-meter band?
A. 28000 - 29700-kHz
B. 28025 - 29700-kHz
C. 28100 - 29600-kHz
D. 28125 - 29600-kHz

ANSWER A: As a General Class operator, you have complete access to the entire 10-meter band from 28.0 MHz to 29.7 MHz. If you ever wondered where FM may be used on the worldwide frequencies, switch to FM and operate simplex at 29.6 MHz. [97.301d]

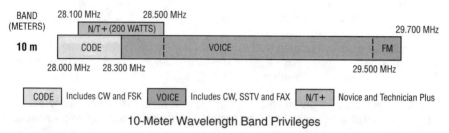

10-Meter Wavelength Band Privileges

G1A09 As a General class control operator at a Novice station, how must you identify the Novice station when transmitting on 7250-kHz?
A. With your call sign, followed by the word "controlling" and the Novice call sign
B. With the Novice call sign, followed by the slant bar "/" (or any suitable word) and your own call sign
C. With your call sign, followed by the slant bar "/" (or any suitable word) and the Novice call sign
D. A Novice station should not be operated on 7250-kHz, even with a General control operator

ANSWER B: Under this scenario, you become the control operator on General frequencies with your General license talking over the Novice operator's equipment. When you ID, say the Novice call sign first, followed by the slant bar or any suitable word, and then your own call sign. This will indicate the station you are using, and your own call letters will show you are acting as a control operator on General frequencies. Got it? Their call sign first, then your call sign when operating at their station. [97.119e]

G1A10 Under what circumstances may a 10-meter repeater retransmit the 2-meter signal from a Technician class operator?
A. Under no circumstances
B. Only if the station on 10 meters is operating under a Special Temporary Authorization allowing such retransmission
C. Only during an FCC-declared general state of communications emergency
D. Only if the 10-meter control operator holds at least a General class license

ANSWER D: 10 meter repeaters may only operate between 29.5 and 29.7 MHz. Technician Class operators have no privileges on these frequencies. However, you can set up your home station as a cross-band relay system. This could allow a Technician on the 2-meter band to end up transmitting and receiving on the 10-meter band. Think of all the excitement you can give Technician Class operators on 2 meters when the 10-meter band is open for worldwide skywave communications. This is perfectly legal to do providing you stay at the control point of your station. You may never leave the relay station unattended without a General Class, or higher, control operator on active duty at the control point. [97.205a]

G1A11 What kind of amateur station simultaneously retransmits the signals of other stations on a different channel?
    A. Repeater station
    B. Space station
    C. Telecommand station
    D. Relay station
ANSWER A: An amateur station that automatically and simultaneously retransmits other amateur stations is called a repeater station. Watch out for Answer D—the official name is a "repeater." [97.3a37]

G1A12 What name is given to a form of interference that seriously degrades, obstructs or repeatedly interrupts a radiocommunication service?
    A. Intentional interference
    B. Harmful interference
    C. Adjacent interference
    D. Disruptive interference
ANSWER B: If a radio operator obstructs or repeatedly interrupts a radio call, the FCC rules call this "harmful" interference. As you study for your General Class written exam, you will find that the incorrect distracters are sometimes pretty close to the most correct answer, so be sure to look at the incorrect answers, too, while preparing for your upcoming General Class exam. [97.3a22]

G1A13 What types of messages may be transmitted by an amateur station to a foreign country for a third party?
    A. Messages for which the amateur operator is paid
    B. Messages facilitating the business affairs of any party
    C. Messages of a technical nature or remarks of a personal character
    D. No messages may be transmitted to foreign countries for third
       parties
ANSWER C: Before you transmit third-party communications to a foreign country, double check that we have a third-party agreement with that nation. The Appendix of this book includes a list of countries with which the U.S. has a third-party agreement. Make sure that the communications are of a personal or technical nature. Business is not allowed, nor can you be paid for handling third-party traffic. [97.115, 97.117]

G1B Antenna structure limitations; good engineering and good amateur practice; beacon operation; restricted operation; retransmitting radio signals

G1B01 Up to what height above the ground may you install an antenna structure without needing FCC approval unless your station is in close proximity to an airport as defined in the FCC Rules?
    A. 50 feet
    B. 100 feet

C. 200 feet

D. 300 feet

ANSWER C: The FCC works closely with the FAA when it comes to towers taller than 200 feet. Although you do not need FCC approval for towers under 200 feet, you may need approval from your city or homeowner's association. [97.15a]

G1B02 If the FCC Rules DO NOT specifically cover a situation, how must you operate your amateur station?

A. In accordance with general licensee operator principles

B. In accordance with good engineering and good amateur practice

C. In accordance with practices adopted by the Institute of Electrical and Electronics Engineers

D. In accordance with procedures set forth by the International Amateur Radio Union

ANSWER B: Every so often you may run into an amateur radio question that is not really answered in the Part 97 rules. Good amateur practice and good engineering practice is how most hams will handle this situation. [97.101a]

G1B03 Which of the following types of stations may normally transmit only one-way communications?

A. Repeater station

B. Beacon station

C. HF station

D. VHF station

ANSWER B: Beacon stations are important for the study of propagation from the ionosphere as well as the atmosphere. Always try to stay clear of beacon stations when selecting a frequency on which to transmit. Beacon stations are found at 14.10 MHz, 28.2-28.3 MHz, and up on the 2-meter band below 144.3 MHz. These are one-way transmissions. [97.203g]

G1B04 Which of the following does NOT need to be true if an amateur station gathers news information for broadcast purposes?

A. The information is more quickly transmitted by Amateur Radio

B. The information must involve the immediate safety of life of individuals or the immediate protection of property

C. The information must be directly related to the event

D. The information cannot be transmitted by other means

ANSWER A: Amateur Radio may generally NOT be used for gathering news for broadcast purposes. Even though the information is transmitted more quickly by Amateur Radio, this alone specifically does NOT make it legal. [97.113b]

G1B05 Under what limited circumstances may music be transmitted by an amateur station?

A. When it produces no dissonances or spurious emissions

B. When it is used to jam an illegal transmission

C. When it is transmitted on frequencies above 1215 MHz

D. When it is an incidental part of a space shuttle retransmission

ANSWER D: About the only music you will ever hear on the ham bands is limited to some of the audio feeds from the space shuttle retransmissions where they sometimes wake up the crew with reveille, or sing "Happy Birthday" to them in outer space. All other forms of music are not allowed. [97.113e]

G1B06 When may an amateur station in two-way communication transmit a message in a secret code in order to obscure the meaning of the communication?
A. When transmitting above 450 MHz
B. During contests
C. Never
D. During a declared communications emergency

ANSWER C: Secret codes to obscure the meaning of a communication are not allowed—ever. Morse code and Q-codes are not considered secret. [97.113a4]

G1B07 What are the restrictions on the use of abbreviations or procedural signals in the amateur service?
A. There are no restrictions
B. They may be used if they do not obscure the meaning of a message
C. They are not permitted because they obscure the meaning of a message to FCC monitoring stations
D. Only "10-codes" are permitted

ANSWER B: Common abbreviations on the ham bands are perfectly acceptable, such as "73," "QRZ?," or "Please QSL." Popular Q signals are given in the Appendix. The following is a list of common prowords: [97.113a4]

Proword	Meaning	Proword	Meaning
Affirmative	Yes	Number	Message number (in numerals) follows
All after	Say again all after _____		
All before	Say again all before _____	Out	End of transmission, no answer required or expected
Break	Used to separate message heading, text and ending	Over	End of transmission, answer is expected. Go ahead. Transmit.
Break	Stop transmitting	Roger	I have received your transmission satisfactorily
Correct	That is correct		
Figures	Numerals follow	Say again	Repeat
From	Originator follows	Slant	Slant bar
Groups	Numeral(s) indicating number of text words follows	This is	This transmission is from the station whose call sign follows
Incorrect	That is incorrect	Time	File time or date-time group of the message follows
Initial	Single letter follows		
I say again	I repeat	To	Addressee follows
I spell	Phonetic spelling follows	Wait	Short pause
Message follows	A message which requires recording follows	Wait out	Long pause
		Word after	Say again word after _____
More to follow	I have more traffic for you	Word before	Say again word before _____
Negative	No, not received		

MARS-Army Radiotelephone Prowords

G1B08 When are codes or ciphers permitted in two-way domestic amateur communications?
A. Never, if intended to obscure meaning
B. During contests
C. During nationally declared emergencies
D. On frequencies above 2.3-GHz
ANSWER A: Secret codes and ciphers are not allowed on ham radio. [97.113a4]

G1B09 When are codes or ciphers permitted in two-way international amateur communications?
A. Never, if intended to obscure meaning
B. During contests
C. During internationally declared emergencies
D. On frequencies above 2.3-GHz
ANSWER A: Codes and ciphers are never permitted in domestic or international amateur radio communications. [97.113a4]

G1B10 Which of the following amateur transmissions is NOT prohibited by the FCC Rules?
A. The playing of music
B. The use of obscene or indecent words
C. False or deceptive messages or signals
D. Retransmission of space shuttle communications
ANSWER D: FCC rules allow for the retransmission of space shuttle communications on ham frequencies. This is a great way to get kids interested in what's happening over the airwaves. [97.113a4, 97.113e]

G1B11 What should you do to keep your station from retransmitting music or signals from a non-amateur station?
A. Turn up the volume of your transceiver
B. Speak closer to the microphone to increase your signal strength
C. Turn down the volume of background audio
D. Adjust your transceiver noise blanker
ANSWER C: If you are driving down the road with your car radio tuned to an FM music station, turn down the FM music. Music is not allowed over the airwaves unless you are flying the space shuttle! [97.113a4, 97.113e]

G1C Transmitter power standards; type acceptance of external RF power amplifiers; standards for type acceptance of external RF power amplifiers; HF data emission standards

G1C01 What is the maximum transmitting power an amateur station may use on 3690-kHz?
A. 200 watts PEP output
B. 1000 watts PEP output
C. 1500 watts PEP output
D. The minimum power necessary to carry out the desired communications with a maximum of 2000 watts PEP output
ANSWER A: Here are a series of questions where you will need to recall Novice CW privileges. Remember, even though you may now have new General Class privileges for 1500 watts PEP output, you may not run any more than 200 watts

PEP output on any high-frequency Novice band. Is 3690 kHz a Novice frequency? Yes; 3675 to 3725 kHz is restricted to 200 watts PEP output maximum. [97.313c1] See question G1A02.

G1C02 What is the maximum transmitting power an amateur station may use on 7080-kHz?
    A. 200 watts PEP output
    B. 1000 watts PEP output
    C. 1500 watts PEP output
    D. 2000 watts PEP output
ANSWER C: Is this within the Novice portion of the 40-meter band? Nope, so 1500 watts PEP output is allowed. [97.313a,b] See question G1A03.

G1C03 What is the maximum transmitting power an amateur station may use on 10.140 MHz?
    A. 200 watts PEP output
    B. 1000 watts PEP output
    C. 1500 watts PEP output
    D. 2000 watts PEP output
ANSWER A: Here is a special case, on the 30-meter band, where only 200 watts PEP output is allowed. [97.313c1] See question G1A04.

G1C04 What is the maximum transmitting power an amateur station may use on 21.150 MHz?
    A. 200 watts PEP output
    B. 1000 watts PEP output
    C. 1500 watts PEP output
    D. 2000 watts PEP output
ANSWER A: 21.150 MHz is right in the middle of the Novice sub-band, so everyone must cut back their power to no more than 200 watts PEP output. [97.313c1] See question G1A06.

G1C05 What is the maximum transmitting power an amateur station may use on 24.950 MHz?
    A. 200 watts PEP output
    B. 1000 watts PEP output
    C. 1500 watts PEP output
    D. 2000 watts PEP output
ANSWER C: You can run the legal limit 1500 watts PEP output on the 12-meter band. [97.313a,b] See question G1A07.

G1C06 External RF power amplifiers designed to operate below what frequency may require FCC type acceptance?
    A. 28 MHz
    B. 35 MHz
    C. 50 MHz
    D. 144 MHz
ANSWER D: Power amplifiers, sometimes called linears, require FCC type acceptance for operation below 144 MHz. Most amateur radio service power amplifiers may need to be modified by the hams themselves to include the 10-meter band, right next to the 11-meter CB band. [97.315a]

G1C07 Without a grant of FCC type acceptance, how many external RF amplifiers of a given design capable of operation below 144 MHz may you build or modify in one calendar year?
  A. None
  B. 1
  C. 5
  D. 10
ANSWER B: Amateur operators are encouraged to build their own power amplifier for use below 144 MHz. If you build no more than one a year, it does not require FCC type acceptance. [97.315a]

G1C08 Which of the following standards must be met if FCC type acceptance of an external RF amplifier is required?
  A. The amplifier must not be able to amplify a 28-MHz signal to more than ten times the input power
  B. The amplifier must not be capable of reaching its designed output power when driven with less than 50 watts
  C. The amplifier must not be able to be operated for more than ten minutes without a time delay circuit
  D. The amplifier must not be able to be modified by an amateur operator
ANSWER B: The FCC will not allow low-power input power amplifiers because they might be used by CB radio operators to increase the output from their 5-watt CB sets. The amplifier must be capable of reaching its designed output power with 50 watts or more of drive power. [97.317a3]

G1C09 Which of the following would NOT disqualify an external RF power amplifier from being granted FCC type acceptance?
  A. The capability of being modified by the operator for use outside the amateur bands
  B. The capability of achieving full output power when driven with less than 50 watts
  C. The capability of achieving full output power on amateur frequencies between 24 and 35 MHz
  D. The capability of being switched by the operator to all amateur frequencies below 24 MHz
ANSWER D: Most power amplifiers cover all ham bands below 24 MHz. New, out of the box, they will not go above 24 MHz to prevent CB radio operators from illegally using these devices. [97.317b,c]

G1C10 What is the maximum symbol rate permitted for packet emissions below 28 MHz?
  A. 300 bauds
  B. 1200 bauds
  C. 19.6 kilobauds
  D. 56 kilobauds
ANSWER A: Packet emissions below 28 MHz must creep along no faster than 300 baud. This slow symbol rate is required to minimize bandwidth allocation on the very crowded high-frequency bands. [97.305c, 97.307f3]

G1C11 What is the maximum symbol rate permitted for RTTY emissions below 28 MHz?
A. 56 kilobauds
B. 19.6 kilobauds
C. 1200 bauds
D. 300 bauds
ANSWER D: Same thing for RTTY emissions—no faster than 300 baud below 10 meters. [97.305c, 97.307f3]

G1D Examination element preparation; examination administration; temporary station identification

G1D01 What telegraphy examination elements may you prepare if you hold a General class license?
A. None
B. Element 1A only
C. Element 1B only
D. Elements 1A and 1B
ANSWER B: When you pass your General Class license, get set to join your local volunteer examination team, accredited by a regional or national VEC. Three General Class operators may administer Novice and Technician Class examinations at an accredited VE session. However, Generals can only make up the Novice telegraphy code test, Element 1A, at 5 wpm. [97.507a2]

G1D02 What written examination elements may you prepare if you hold a General class license?
A. None
B. Element 2 only
C. Elements 2 and 3A
D. Elements 2, 3A and 3B
ANSWER C: As a General Class licensee, you may prepare and administer Novice, Element 2, and Technician, Element 3A, examinations as part of an accredited VE team. [97.507a2,3]

G1D03 What license examinations may you administer if you hold a General class license?
A. None
B. Novice only
C. Novice, Technician and Technician Plus
D. Novice, Technician and General
ANSWER C: The Novice, Technician, and Technician-Plus Class examinations are yours to administer once you develop a three-member General Class VE team. You will find a list of VECs in the back of this book. As soon as your new General Class license arrives, join up! [97.509b3i]

G1D04 What minimum examination elements must an applicant pass for a Novice license?
A. Element 2 only
B. Elements 1A and 2
C. Elements 2 and 3A
D. Elements 1A, 2 and 3A

ANSWER B: For the Novice license, applicants must pass an Element 1A 5-wpm code test and an Element 2 written theory examination. [97.501f]

G1D05 What minimum examination elements must an applicant pass for a Technician license?
 A. Element 2 only
 B. Elements 1A and 2
 C. Elements 2 and 3A
 D. Elements 1A, 2 and 3A

ANSWER C: The Technician license applicant must pass the written requirements for Novice Element 2 and Technician Element 3A for a no-code Technician Class license. [97.501e]

G1D06 What minimum examination elements must an applicant pass for a Technician Plus license?
 A. Element 2 only
 B. Elements 1A and 2
 C. Elements 2 and 3A
 D. Elements 1A, 2 and 3A

ANSWER D: For high-frequency privileges on 80 meters, 40 meters, 15 meters, and 10 meters, the Technician-Plus (plus the code) applicant will need to pass a Novice Element 1A code test, a Novice written theory examination on Element 2, and Technician written theory examination on Element 3A. [97.501d]

G1D07 What are the requirements for administering Novice examinations?
 A. Three VEC-accredited General class or higher VEs must be present
 B. Two VEC-accredited General class or higher VEs must be present
 C. Two General class or higher VEs must be present, but only one need be VEC accredited
 D. Any two General class or higher VEs must be present

ANSWER A: Three General Class or higher Volunteer Examiners (VEs) accredited by a Volunteer Examiner Coordinate (VEC) are required to administer the Novice examination. No longer may two General Class hams give the Novice examinations. [97.509a,b]

G1D08 When may you participate as an administering Volunteer Examiner (VE) for a Novice license examination?
 A. Once you have notified the FCC that you want to give an examination
 B. Once you have a Certificate of Successful Completion of Examination (CSCE) for General class
 C. Once you have prepared telegraphy and written examinations for the Novice license, or obtained them from a qualified supplier
 D. Once you have been granted your FCC General class or higher license and received your VEC accreditation

ANSWER D: You may start your VE General Class team as soon as all three of you hold an FCC-issued General Class or higher license, and each of you has been accredited by a regional or national VEC. You apply for accreditation by writing the VEC of your choice (a list can be found in the Appendix) and asking for accreditation materials. [97.509b3i]

G1D09 If you are a Technician licensee with a Certificate of Successful Completion of Examination (CSCE) for General privileges, how do you identify your station when transmitting on 14.035 MHz?
- A. You must give your call sign and the location of the VE examination where you obtained the CSCE
- B. You must give your call sign, followed by the slant mark "/," followed by the identifier "AG"
- C. You may not operate on 14.035 MHz until your new license arrives
- D. No special form of identification is needed

ANSWER B: Good news! You can go on the air immediately with your new General Class privileges if you presently hold a Technician Class license. You would give your call sign, followed by the slant mark when operating on code, followed by the identifier "AG." You would say, "Temporary AG" on the world-wide General Class bands when operating on SSB. [97.119f2]

G1D10 If you are a Technician licensee with a Certificate of Successful Completion of Examination (CSCE) for General privileges, how do you identify your station when transmitting phone emissions on 14.325 MHz?
- A. No special form of identification is needed
- B. You may not operate on 14.325 MHz until your new license arrives
- C. You must give your call sign, followed by any suitable word that denotes the slant mark and the identifier "AG"
- D. You must give your call sign and the location of the VE examination where you obtained the CSCE

ANSWER C: Simply give your call sign, followed by the suitable word "temporary," and the identifier "AG." [97.119f2]

G1D11 If you are a Technician licensee with a Certificate of Successful Completion of Examination (CSCE) for General privileges, when must you add the special identifier "AG" after your call sign?
- A. Whenever you operate using your new frequency privileges
- B. Whenever you operate
- C. Whenever you operate using Technician frequency privileges
- D. A special identifier is not required as long as your General class license application has been filed with the FCC

ANSWER A: You must use the temporary "AG" until your actual new license arrives whenever you are operating on General Class frequencies. [97.119f2]

SUBELEMENT G2 — OPERATING PROCEDURES   [3 exam questions - 3 topic groups]

G2A Phone; RTTY; repeater; VOX and full break-in CW

G2A01 Which sideband is commonly used for 20-meter phone operation?
- A. Upper
- B. Lower
- C. Amplitude compandored
- D. Double

ANSWER A: We normally use upper sideband (USB) for all voice emissions on 20 meters, 17 meters, 15 meters, 12 meters, 10 meters, and on all of the VHF and UHF weak-signal portions of the bands.

G2A02 Which sideband is commonly used on 3925-kHz for phone operation?
   A. Upper
   B. Lower
   C. Amplitude compandored
   D. Double

ANSWER B: We use lower sideband (LSB) on 160 meters, 80 meters, and 40 meters. And while it is not absolutely illegal to use lower sideband on 20 meters and shorter wavelength bands, good operating procedure would always indicate "go with the flow" and use the proper sideband.

G2A03 In what segment of the 80-meter band do most RTTY transmissions take place?
   A. 3580 - 3620-kHz
   B. 3500 - 3525-kHz
   C. 3700 - 3750-kHz
   D. 3775 - 3825-kHz

ANSWER A: If you have a worldwide ham set and a home computer, add a relatively simple digital decoder and listen to and watch the RTTY transmissions between 3580 kHz to 3620 kHz.

G2A04 In what segment of the 20-meter band do most RTTY transmissions take place?
   A. 14.000 - 14.050 MHz
   B. 14.070 - 14.095 MHz
   C. 14.150 - 14.225 MHz
   D. 14.275 - 14.350 MHz

ANSWER B: Most RTTY transmissions on the 20-meter band are found between 14.070 MHz to 14.095 MHz, a 25 kHz RTTY "window." Use the LSB switch to tune in 20-meter RTTY stations using a digital decoder.

G2A05 What is the Baudot code?
   A. A 7-bit code, with start, stop and parity bits
   B. A 7-bit code in which each character has four mark and three space bits
   C. A 5-bit code, with additional start and stop bits
   D. A 6-bit code, with additional start, stop and parity bits

ANSWER C: You pronounce baudot as "baa doe." The "t" is silent. If you take the "t" out of baudot, it has just five letters in the word. Baudot is a 5-bit code used for RTTY radioteleprinter transmissions. Most worldwide ham stations operate at a speed of 45 baud with a 170-Hz shift between the mark and space tones.

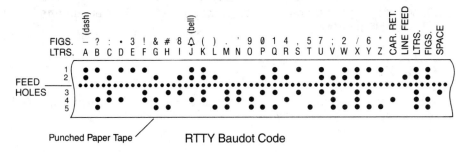

Punched Paper Tape — RTTY Baudot Code

G2A06 What is ASCII?

A. A 7-bit code, with additional start, stop and parity bits
B. A 7-bit code in which each character has four mark and three space bits
C. A 5-bit code, with additional start and stop bits
D. A 5-bit code in which each character has three mark and two space bits

ANSWER A: ASCII stands for American Standard Code for Information Interchange. This type of radioteleprinter communication runs faster, and offers upper and lower case printing. Answer A has "parity bits" that makes it the correct answer—the parity bits allow the computer to detect received errors in the transmission.

Bit Position

| | | | | | | | | 0 | 1 | 0 | 1 | 1 | 0 | 0 | 1 |
| | | | | | | | | 0 | 0 | 1 | 1 | 1 | 1 | 0 | 0 |
1	2	3	4	5	6	7		1	1	1	1	0	0	0	0
0	0	0	0					@	P	`	p	0	sp	NUL	DLE
1	0	0	0					A	Q	a	q	1	!	SOH	DC1
0	1	0	0					B	R	b	r	2	"	STX	DC2
1	1	0	0					C	S	c	s	3	#	ETX	DC3
0	0	1	0					D	T	d	t	4	$	EOT	DC4
1	0	1	0					E	U	e	u	5	%	ENQ	NAK
0	1	1	0					F	V	f	v	6	&	ACK	SYN
1	1	1	0					G	W	g	w	7	'	BEL	ETB
0	0	0	1					H	X	h	x	8	(	BS	CAN
1	0	0	1					I	Y	i	y	9	)	HT	EM
0	1	0	1					J	Z	j	z	:	*	LF	SUB
1	1	0	1					K	[	k	{	;	+	VT	ESC
0	0	1	1					L	\	l			<	,	FF	FS
1	0	1	1					M	]	m	}	=	−	CR	GS
0	1	1	1					N	^	n	~	>	.	SO	RS
1	1	1	1					O	—	o	DEL	?	/	SI	US

American Standard Code for Information Interchange (ASCII)

Source: *Digital Communications with Packet Radio*, © 1988 Master Publishing, Inc., Lincolnwood, IL

G2A07 What is the most common frequency shift for RTTY emissions in the amateur HF bands?

A. 85 Hz
B. 170 Hz
C. 425 Hz
D. 850 Hz

ANSWER B: Almost all ham radio transmissions use the 170-Hz shift. Commercial broadcast stations on shortwave use larger frequency shifts.

G2A08 What are the two major AMTOR operating modes?
  A. Mode AM and Mode TR
  B. Mode A (ARQ) and Mode B (FEC)
  C. Mode C (CRQ) and Mode D (DEC)
  D. Mode SELCAL and Mode LISTEN
ANSWER B: When you listen to AMTOR (AMateur Telex Over Radio), it may sound like two birds chirping. What you are hearing are two computers communicating back and forth, checking for errors. ARQ stands for Automatic Repeat Request. FEC stands for Forward Error Correction.

G2A09 What is the usual input/output frequency separation for a 10-meter station in repeater operation?
  A. 100-kHz
  B. 600-kHz
  C. 1.6 MHz
  D. 170 MHz
ANSWER A: That's right, there ARE repeaters on the 10-meter band. Switch to FM, and tune between 29.5 MHz to 29.7 MHz. Input is low, and output is high, separated by a 100-kHz split. Most repeaters also use CTCSS (continuous tone-coded squelch system).

G2A10 What is the circuit called that causes a transmitter to automatically transmit when an operator speaks into its microphone?
  A. VXO
  B. VOX
  C. VCO
  D. VFO
ANSWER B: VOX stands for "voice operated relay," and it will trigger your transceiver on the air as soon as you speak into the microphone. We normally use VOX only for base station operation.

G2A11 Which of the following describes full break-in telegraphy?
  A. Breaking stations send the Morse code prosign BK
  B. Automatic keyers are used to send Morse code instead of hand keys
  C. An operator must activate a manual send/receive switch before and after every transmission
  D. Incoming signals are received between transmitted key pulses
ANSWER D: Full break-in telegraphy is abbreviated "QSK." This setting allows your transceiver to immediately pop back to the receive mode in between all dots and dashes being sent. A high-speed operator can then listen to the frequency to ensure no one is trying to interrupt during the CW transmission.

G2B Operating courtesy; antenna orientation and HF operations, including logging practices; ITU Regions

G2B01 If you are the net control station of a daily HF net, what should you do if the frequency on which you normally meet is in use just before the net begins?
  A. Reduce your output power and start the net as usual
  B. Increase your power output so that net participants will be able to hear you over the existing activity

C. Cancel the net for that day

D. Conduct the net on a frequency 3 to 5-kHz away from the regular net frequency

ANSWER D: As a new General Class operator, you are going to find many daytime and evening nets on the worldwide frequencies conducted on a daily basis. Every so often the frequency is in use before the net begins. Courteous net controllers may ask the operating stations whether or not the net can go on this same frequency while the two stations previously operating stand by. An alternate method would be to conduct the net on a nearby frequency, no closer than 3 to 5 kHz away from the regular net frequency.

G2B02 If a net is about to begin on a frequency which you and another station are using, what should you do?

A. As a courtesy to the net, move to a different frequency

B. Increase your power output to ensure that all net participants can hear you

C. Transmit as long as possible on the frequency so that no other stations may use it

D. Turn off your radio

ANSWER A: If you are asked to move prior to a net beginning, as a courtesy to all ham operators, shift off the frequency.

G2B03 If propagation changes during your contact and you notice increasing interference from other activity on the same frequency, what should you do?

A. Tell the interfering stations to change frequency, since you were there first

B. Report the interference to your local Amateur Auxiliary Coordinator

C. Turn on your amplifier to overcome the interference

D. Move your contact to another frequency

ANSWER D: On the worldwide General Class ham bands, propagation will sometimes cause stations on the same frequency to all of a sudden come in right on top of your ongoing contact. Be a good ham and move your contact to another frequency, if you can, to avoid the interference.

G2B04 When selecting a CW transmitting frequency, what minimum frequency separation from a contact in progress should you allow to minimize interference?

A. 5 to 50 Hz

B. 150 to 500 Hz

C. 1 to 3 kHz

D. 3 to 6 kHz

ANSWER B: When operating CW, try to separate yourself from other CW transmissions by at least 150 Hz to 500 Hz. This will give your CW tone a distinct tonal difference from the other station, and hopefully will not cause interference.

G2B05 When selecting a single-sideband phone transmitting frequency, what minimum frequency separation from a contact in progress should you allow (between suppressed carriers) to minimize interference?

A. 150 to 500 Hz

B. Approximately 3 kHz

C. Approximately 6 kHz

D. Approximately 10 kHz

ANSWER B: When operating single sideband, your emission will take up approximately 3 kHz of bandwidth. Always stay at least 3 kHz away from any other station on the air that is using an adjacent frequency.

G2B06 When selecting a RTTY transmitting frequency, what minimum frequency separation from a contact in progress should you allow (center to center) to minimize interference?

A. 60 Hz

B. 250 to 500 Hz

C. Approximately 3 kHz

D. Approximately 6 kHz

ANSWER B: On RTTY, similar to CW, stay at least 250 Hz to 500 Hz away from an ongoing communication.

G2B07 What is an azimuthal map?

A. A map projection centered on the North Pole

B. A map projection centered on a particular location, used to determine the shortest path between points on the surface of the earth

C. A map that shows the angle at which an amateur satellite crosses the equator

D. A map that shows the number of degrees longitude that an amateur satellite appears to move westward at the equator with each orbit

ANSWER B: Long-range communications do not necessarily go in straight lines. When we navigate our signals around the world, we need a chart that takes into account the curvature of the earth. The azimuthal map will determine the shortest path between your station and that rare DX station.

G2B08 What is the most useful type of map to use when orienting a directional HF antenna toward a distant station?

A. Azimuthal

B. Mercator

C. Polar projection

D. Topographical

ANSWER A: An azimuthal map; see explanation at previous question G2B07.

G2B09 A directional antenna pointed in the long-path direction to another station is generally oriented how many degrees from its short-path heading?

A. 45 degrees

B. 90 degrees

C. 180 degrees

D. 270 degrees

ANSWER C: Some ionospheric conditions may allow you to establish communications with a distant station on General Class worldwide frequencies over a longer path around the world than the direct short path. If you hear the station with an echo, try turning your beam antenna 180 degrees in the opposite direction from the short path direction to see whether or not the station will come in better along the long path. The echo you hear is the difference in the transmission delay between long path and short path transmissions.

G2B10 What is a band plan?

    A. A voluntary guideline beyond the divisions established by the FCC for using different operating modes within an amateur band

    B. A guideline from the FCC for making amateur frequency band allocations

    C. A plan of operating schedules within an amateur band published by the FCC

    D. A plan devised by a club to best use a frequency band during a contest

ANSWER A: The worldwide General Class bands have specific designated areas where different operating modes take place within the band. This is called a band plan, and there are different areas reserved within each band for specific types of emissions. It's important to know the band plan before transmitting on any Amateur Radio frequency. Just because you may have earned new privileges for a particular portion of the band does not necessarily mean you may operate any way you want on that band. Certain segments of the world-wide band may be reserved for working foreign stations. There are other segments on the worldwide band for slow-scan television. There are still other segments for satellite reception.

    You should do a lot of listening with your new General Class privileges, and only transmit to another SSB station when you hear them coming in loud and clear. This way you won't accidentally transmit voice on a portion of the band that might be reserved for, let's say, slow-scan television within the voice portion of the band. Remember, every band has a band plan and you must abide by the recommended band usage.

G2B11 In which International Telecommunication Union Region is the continental United States?

    A. Region 1

    B. Region 2

    C. Region 3

    D. Region 4

ANSWER B: In the United States, we are in Region 2. If you are reading this book in the South Seas, you are in Region 3. Or maybe you are studying for your General Class examination in Europe—if so, your are in Region 1.

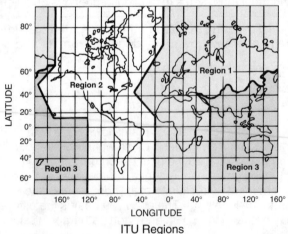

ITU Regions

G2C Emergencies, including drills; communications and amateur auxiliary to the FCC's Compliance and Information Bureau

G2C01 What means may an amateur station in distress use to attract attention, make known its condition and location, and obtain assistance?
   A. Only Morse code signals sent on internationally recognized emergency channels
   B. Any means of radiocommunication, but only on internationally recognized emergency channels
   C. Any means of radiocommunication
   D. Only those means of radiocommunication for which the station is licensed
ANSWER C: In an emergency, you are not confined only to General Class frequencies. In an emergency, you could slide down to the Extra Class portion of the band and signal for help if this is the only area where you hear activity. NEVER would you consider using a hand-held transceiver on a police frequency in an emergency where you might be able to switch to other frequencies to get help. Police channels are absolutely taboo for emergency ham transmissions.

G2C02 During a disaster in the US, when may an amateur station make transmissions necessary to meet essential communication needs and assist relief operations?
   A. When normal communication systems are overloaded, damaged or disrupted
   B. Only when the local RACES net is activated
   C. Never; only official emergency stations may transmit in a disaster
   D. When normal communication systems are working but are not convenient
ANSWER A: Hams usually rise to the occasion and perform very well when they are needed to handle emergency, health and welfare traffic.

G2C03 If a disaster disrupts normal communications in your area, what may the FCC do?
   A. Declare a temporary state of communication emergency
   B. Temporarily seize your equipment for use in disaster communications
   C. Order all stations across the country to stop transmitting at once
   D. Nothing until the President declares the area a disaster area
ANSWER A: In a major emergency, the FCC could declare a temporary state of communications emergency, restricting the radio traffic to only emergency communications.

G2C04 If a disaster disrupts normal communications in an area, what would the FCC include in any notice of a temporary state of communication emergency?
   A. Any additional test questions needed for the licensing of amateur emergency communications workers
   B. A list of organizations authorized to temporarily seize your equipment for disaster communications

C. Any special conditions requiring the use of noncommercial power systems

D. Any special conditions and special rules to be observed by stations during the emergency

ANSWER D: If someone comes on the air and tells you to stand by for emergency-only communications, don't transmit. Emergency traffic always has priority.

G2C05 During an emergency, what power output limitations must be observed by a station in distress?

A. 200 watts PEP

B. 1500 watts PEP

C. 1000 watts PEP during daylight hours, reduced to 200 watts PEP during the night

D. There are no limitations during an emergency

ANSWER D: In an emergency, there are no power output limitations. However, most worldwide transmissions stay "barefoot"—no linear amplifier required—because there may be severe power outages. If the station is operating from battery supply only, it will want to use minimum power for clear communications.

G2C06 During a disaster in the US, what frequencies may be used to obtain assistance?

A. Only frequencies in the 80-meter band

B. Only frequencies in the 40-meter band

C. Any frequency

D. Any United Nations approved frequency

ANSWER C: During a disaster, any station handling emergency traffic may use any frequency to obtain assistance.

G2C07 If you are communicating with another amateur station and hear a station in distress break in, what should you do?

A. Continue your communication because you were on frequency first

B. Acknowledge the station in distress and determine its location and what assistance may be needed

C. Change to a different frequency so the station in distress may have a clear channel to call for assistance

D. Immediately cease all transmissions because stations in distress have emergency rights to the frequency

ANSWER B: Act quickly to handle a station in distress. Find out *WHO* is in distress, *WHERE* they are located, and *WHAT* assistance may be needed. If it's a boat, find out how many persons are on board and instruct everyone to put on their personal floatation device.

G2C08 Why do stations in the Radio Amateur Civil Emergency Service (RACES) participate in training tests and drills?

A. To practice orderly and efficient operations for the civil defense organization they serve

B. To ensure that members attend monthly on-the-air meetings

C. To ensure that RACES members are able to conduct tests and drills

D. To acquaint members of RACES with other members they may meet in an emergency

ANSWER A: Amateur stations participating in RACES drills are part of our civil defense organization.

G2C09 What type of messages may be transmitted to an amateur station in a foreign country?
   A. Messages of any type
   B. Messages that are not religious, political, or patriotic in nature
   C. Messages of a technical nature or personal remarks of relative unimportance
   D. Messages of any type, but only if the foreign country has a third-party communications agreement with the US

ANSWER C: Your new General Class privileges will give you regular communications to stations in foreign countries. When talking to a foreign amateur operator, limit your transmissions to a technical discussion or to personal remarks of relative unimportance. It's perfectly okay to speak their language, too—but keep your transmission fun, and avoid any political discussions.

G2C10 What is the Amateur Auxiliary to the FCC's Compliance and Information Bureau?
   A. Amateur volunteers who are formally enlisted to monitor the airwaves for rules violations
   B. Amateur volunteers who conduct amateur licensing examinations
   C. Amateur volunteers who conduct frequency coordination for amateur VHF repeaters
   D. Amateur volunteers who use their station equipment to help civil defense organizations in times of emergency

ANSWER A: The Amateur Auxiliary is made up of volunteer hams who are formally enlisted to monitor the airwaves for rule violations, and who report violations to the local FCC Compliance and Information Bureau office.

G2C11 What are the objectives of the Amateur Auxiliary to the FCC's Compliance and Information Bureau?
   A. To conduct efficient and orderly amateur licensing examinations
   B. To encourage amateur self-regulation and compliance with the rules
   C. To coordinate repeaters for efficient and orderly spectrum usage
   D. To provide emergency and public safety communications

ANSWER B: The benchmark of the amateur service is self-regulation and compliance with the rules. Hams help other hams stay on the straight and narrow. The FCC has little time nor budget to monitor the amateur bands for rule violations.

Subelement G3 – Radio Wave Propagation   (3 exam questions – 3 topic groups)

G3A Ionospheric disturbances; sunspots and solar radiation

G3A01 What can be done at an amateur station to continue communications during a sudden ionospheric disturbance?
   A. Try a higher frequency
   B. Try the other sideband
   C. Try a different antenna polarization
   D. Try a different frequency shift

ANSWER A: During a SID (sudden ionospheric disturbance), bands like 40 meters and 20 meters develop extremely high noise levels, sometimes greater than S9. Switch up to 15 meters or 10 meters and see if you can hear distant stations during this "radio blackout" period.

G3A02 What effect does a sudden ionospheric disturbance have on the day-time ionospheric propagation of HF radio waves?
   A. It disrupts higher-latitude paths more than lower-latitude paths
   B. It disrupts signals on lower frequencies more than those on higher frequencies
   C. It disrupts communications via satellite more than direct communications
   D. None, only areas on the night side of the earth are affected
ANSWER B: The lower bands, such as 160, 80, 40, and even 20 meters, become so noisy that it is impossible to hear any distant signals coming in from sky waves.

G3A03 How long does it take the increased ultraviolet and X-ray radiation from solar flares to affect radio-wave propagation on the earth?
   A. The effect is almost instantaneous
   B. 1.5 minutes
   C. 8 minutes
   D. 20 to 40 hours
ANSWER C: Ultraviolet radiation travels at the speed of light. It takes 8 minutes for sunlight and ultraviolet rays to reach the earth's ionosphere. Sunspots may quickly appear, and heavy sunspot activity may affect worldwide propagation for up to three days.

G3A04 What is solar flux?
   A. The density of the sun's magnetic field
   B. The radio energy emitted by the sun
   C. The number of sunspots on the side of the sun facing the earth
   D. A measure of the tilt of the earth's ionosphere on the side toward the sun
ANSWER B: We can actually measure the radio noise energy emitted by the sun with special receiving equipment. You can also test your VHF and UHF antenna system by aiming these antennas at the sun and listening to sun noise.

G3A05 What is the solar-flux index?
   A. A measure of solar activity that is taken annually
   B. A measure of solar activity that compares daily readings with results from the last six months
   C. Another name for the American sunspot number
   D. A measure of solar activity that is taken at a specific frequency
ANSWER D: The solar-flux index is measured daily in Ottawa, Canada. Measurements are on the frequency of 2800 MHz late every afternoon. You may tune into the radio propagational forecasts transmitted by WWV at 18 minutes past the hour. Frequencies of 10 and 15 MHz will give you best reception during the day, and 5 MHz may give you best reception at night.

G3A06 What is a geomagnetic disturbance?
A. A sudden drop in the solar-flux index
B. A shifting of the earth's magnetic pole
C. Ripples in the ionosphere
D. A dramatic change in the earth's magnetic field over a short period of time

ANSWER D: When there are major flare ups on the sun, it will change the earth's magnetic field over a short period of time, affecting worldwide radio waves. There is little or no effect on VHF or UHF signals.

G3A07 At which latitudes are propagation paths more sensitive to geomagnetic disturbances?
A. Those greater than 45 degrees latitude
B. Those between 5 and 45 degrees latitude
C. Those near the equator
D. All paths are affected equally

ANSWER A: Do you live north of 45 degrees north? If you do, your location will be more sensitive to geomagnetic disturbances than for the rest of us down here at latitude 33 degrees.

G3A08 What can be the effect of a major geomagnetic storm on radio-wave propagation?
A. Improved high-latitude HF propagation
B. Degraded high-latitude HF propagation
C. Improved ground-wave propagation
D. Improved chances of UHF ducting

ANSWER B: During periods of major geomagnetic disturbances, high-frequency propagation over high-latitude paths will be degraded.

G3A09 What phenomenon has the most effect on radio communication beyond ground-wave or line-of-sight ranges?
A. Solar activity
B. Lunar tidal effects
C. The F1 region of the ionosphere
D. The F2 region of the ionosphere

ANSWER A: Solar activity influences sky-wave communications, but has little affect on ground-wave or line-of-sight ranges.

G3A10 Which two types of radiation from the sun influence propagation?
A. Subaudible-frequency and audio-frequency emissions
B. Electromagnetic and particle emissions
C. Polar-region and equatorial emissions
D. Infrared and gamma-ray emissions

ANSWER B: The electromagnetic rays from the sun influence propagation within 8 minutes of a major disturbance on the face of the sun. Particle emissions, a slower moving mass of radio-interfering noise, may take anywhere from 20 to 40 hours to really give us a second wallop of disturbed conditions. This allows propagation forecasters to get a slight advance warning on upcoming world-wide-band radio disturbances coming our way.

G3A11 When sunspot numbers are high, what is the affect on radio communications?
A. High-frequency radio signals are absorbed
B. Frequencies above 300 MHz become usable for long-distance communication
C. Long-distance communication in the upper HF and lower VHF range is enhanced
D. High-frequency radio signals become weak and distorted

ANSWER C: We are presently on the up side of solar cycle 23. We will continue to see increased band activity until the peak around 2001. With more sunspots, we will have more long-distance communication in the upper HF and lower VHF bands, including 6 meters and sometimes even 2 meters.

G3B Maximum usable frequency; propagation "hops"

G3B01 If the maximum usable frequency (MUF) on the path from Minnesota to France is 24 MHz, which band should offer the best chance for a successful contact?
A. 10 meters
B. 15 meters
C. 20 meters
D. 40 meters

ANSWER B: The 15-meter band, centered on 21.2 MHz, would be just below the maximum usable frequency at 22 MHz. Have a great time talking to Europe.

G3B02 If the maximum usable frequency (MUF) on the path from Ohio to Germany is 17 MHz, which band should offer the best chance for a successful contact?
A. 80 meters
B. 40 meters
C. 20 meters
D. 2 meters

ANSWER C: The 20-meter band, centered around 14.2 MHz, is well within the maximum usable frequency of 17 MHz, so have a great QSO with Germany.

G3B03 If the HF radio-wave propagation (skip) is generally good on the 24-MHz and 28-MHz bands for several days, when might you expect a similar condition to occur?
A. 7 days later
B. 14 days later
C. 28 days later
D. 90 days later

ANSWER C: You will find recurring sky-wave conditions about 28 days later. Ham radio propagation forecasts are generally quite accurate. Subscribe to Amateur Radio monthly publications, which always include propagation forecasts.

G3B04 What is one way to determine if the maximum usable frequency (MUF) is high enough to support 28-MHz propagation between your station and western Europe?
A. Listen for signals on the 10-meter beacon frequency
B. Listen for signals on the 20-meter beacon frequency

C. Listen for signals on the 39-meter broadcast frequency

D. Listen for WWVH time signals on 20 MHz

ANSWER A: Tune between 28.2 MHz to 28.3 MHz on the 10-meter band, listen for continuous beacons, and copy down the call signs. If you hear stations between 28.2 to 28.3 MHz, the band is wide open and propagation is taking place.

G3B05 What usually happens to radio waves with frequencies below the maximum usable frequency (MUF) when they are sent into the ionosphere?

A. They are bent back to the earth

B. They pass through the ionosphere

C. They are completely absorbed by the ionosphere

D. They are bent and trapped in the ionosphere to circle the Earth

ANSWER A: Frequencies below the maximum usable frequency are bent back to earth by the ionosphere. For maximum range, operate as close to MUF as possible.

G3B06 Where would you tune to hear beacons that would help you determine propagation conditions on the 20-meter band?

A. 28.2 MHz

B. 21.1 MHz

C. 14.1 MHz

D. 18.1 MHz

ANSWER C: Propagation beacons transmit on the same frequency over a 3-minute cycle. These automatic beacons will assist you in determining band conditions for 20-, 17-, 15-, 12-, and 10 meters to 18 locations around the world. The following chart lists this very useful CW propagation beacon rotation.

Slot	Country	Call	14.100	18.110	21.150	24.930	28.200	Operator
1	United Nations	4U1UN	00:00	00:10	00:20	00:30	00:40	UNRC
2	Canada	VE8AT	00:10	00:20	00:30	00:40	00:50	RAC
3	USA	W6WX	00:20	00:30	00:40	00:50	01:00	NCDXF
4	Hawaii	KH6WO	00:30	00:40	00:50	01:00	01:10	UHRO
5	New Zealand	ZL	00:40	00:50	01:00	01:10	01:20	NZART
6	Australia	VK8	00:50	01:00	01:10	01:20	01:30	W1A
7	Japan	JA21CY	01:00	01:10	01:20	01:30	01:40	JARL
8	China	BY	01:10	01:20	01:30	01:40	01:50	CRSA
9	Russia	UA	01:20	01:30	01:40	01:50	02:00	TBO
10	Sri Lanka	4S7B	01:30	01:40	01:50	02:00	02:10	RSSL
11	South Africa	ZS6DN	01:40	01:50	02:00	02:10	02:20	ZS6DN
12	Kenya	5Z4B	01:50	02:00	02:10	02:20	02:30	RSK
13	Israel	4X6TU	02:00	02:10	02:20	02:30	02:40	U of Tel Aviv
14	Finland	OH2B	02:10	02:20	02:30	02:40	02:50	U oh Helsinki
15	Madeira	CS3B	02:20	02:30	02:40	02:50	00:00	ARRM
16	Argentina	LU4AA	02:30	02:40	02:50	00:00	00:10	RCA
17	Peru	OA4B	02:40	02:50	00:00	00:10	00:20	RCP
18	Venezuela	YV5B	02:50	00:00	00:10	00:20	00:30	RCV

The 10-second, phase-3, message format is: "W6WX dah-dah-dah-dah"— each "dah" lasts a little more than one second. W6WX is transmitted at 100 watts, then each "dah" is attenuated in order, beginning at 100 watts, then 10 watts, then 1 watt, and finally 0.1 watt.
Courtesy *CQ Magazine*

Radio Beacon Stations

G3B07 During periods of low solar activity, which frequencies are the least reliable for long-distance communication?
A. Frequencies below 3.5 MHz
B. Frequencies near 3.5 MHz
C. Frequencies on or above 10 MHz
D. Frequencies above 20 MHz
ANSWER D: Frequencies above 20 MHz seldom give worldwide sky-wave DXing during periods of low solar activity. We now are in Solar Cycle 23, and our low solar activity is behind us. Peak solar activity is expected in 2002.

G3B08 At what point in the solar cycle does the 20-meter band usually support worldwide propagation during daylight hours?
A. At the summer solstice
B. Only at the maximum point of the solar cycle
C. Only at the minimum point of the solar cycle
D. At any point in the solar cycle
ANSWER D: Good news for a General Class operator! The 20-meter band is always open to sky-wave communications during daylight hours, except for rare occurrences of sudden ionospheric disturbances. This means the 20-meter band will always provide a daytime DX at any point in the solar cycle.

G3B09 What is one characteristic of gray-line propagation?
A. It is very efficient
B. It improves local communications
C. It is very poor
D. It increases D-region absorption
ANSWER A: Gray-line propagation is the brief period of signal enhancement when both distant stations are enjoying simultaneous sunrise and sunset. It is during these twilight hours that some remarkably clear DX (distant) communications take place. There are computer programs that will list favorable directions for gray-line propagation, and some very exotic color computer programs that will actually illustrate simultaneous sunrise and sunset conditions in the world.

G3B10 What is the maximum distance along the Earth's surface that is normally covered in one hop using the F2 region?
A. 180 miles
B. 1200 miles
C. 2500 miles
D. None; the F2 region does not support radio-wave propagation
ANSWER C: The F2 layer is our highest reflective ionospheric region, approximately 250 miles up. This gives worldwide signals their furthest bounce, generally 2500 miles.

| Layers | Day | | Night |
	Summer	Winter	
F2	>250		
F1	90-150		
F		90-150	90-250
E	55-90	55-90	
D	40	40	

Altitudes in Miles of Ionospheric Layers

G3B11 What is the maximum distance along the Earth's surface that is normally covered in one hop using the E region?
  A. 180 miles
  B. 1200 miles
  C. 2500 miles
  D. None of these choices is correct

ANSWER B: The E layer is between 50 and 90 miles up, and because it's closer to earth, high-frequency waves don't bounce as far as they do off of the F layer. E skip is approximately 1200 miles and, during the summertime, "sporadic E" may sometimes "short skip" in as close as 600 miles.

G3C Height of ionospheric regions; critical angle and frequency; HF scatter

G3C01 What is the average height of maximum ionization of the E region?
  A. 45 miles
  B. 70 miles
  C. 200 miles
  D. 1200 miles

ANSWER B: The E layer normally hovers around 70 miles up. During the summer and fall, intensely ionized patches of E-layer ionosphere will sometimes cause signals on 6 meters and even 2 meters to take a hop back to earth.

G3C02 When can the F2 region be expected to reach its maximum height at your location?
  A. At noon during the summer
  B. At midnight during the summer
  C. At dusk in the spring and fall
  D. At noon during the winter

ANSWER A: All of the ionospheric regions are influenced by ultraviolet radiation from the sun. The F2 region is at its ultimate height at noon during the summer.

G3C03 Why is the F2 region mainly responsible for the longest-distance radio-wave propagation?
  A. Because it exists only at night
  B. Because it is the lowest ionospheric region
  C. Because it is the highest ionospheric region
  D. Because it does not absorb radio waves as much as other ionospheric regions

ANSWER C: The higher the altitude of the ionospheric region reflecting the high-frequency radio waves, the greater the radio range.

G3C04 What is the "critical angle" as used in radio-wave propagation?
  A. The lowest takeoff angle that will return a radio wave to the earth under specific ionospheric conditions
  B. The compass direction of a distant station
  C. The compass direction opposite that of a distant station
  D. The highest takeoff angle that will return a radio wave to the earth under specific ionospheric conditions

ANSWER D: Have you ever skipped stones on a lake? There is an angle that you cannot exceed where the stone doesn't skip, but rather penetrates into the water. Radio waves in the ionosphere act similarly; there is a point—the highest take-off angle—that cannot be exceeded or a radio wave will not reflect back to earth. Just remember *"highest take-off angle."*

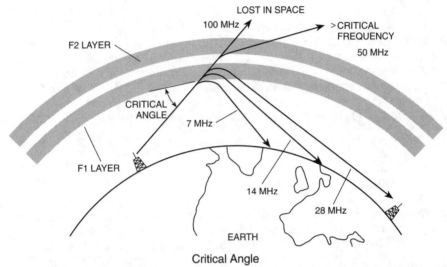

Critical Angle

Source: *Antennas - Selection and Installation*, © 1986 Master Publishing, Inc., Lincolnwood, IL

G3C05 What is the main reason the 160-, 80- and 40-meter amateur bands tend to be useful only for short-distance communications during daylight hours?

    A. Because of a lack of activity
    B. Because of auroral propagation
    C. Because of D-region absorption
    D. Because of magnetic flux

ANSWER C: The "Darn D" layer does more harm than good to medium-frequency and high-frequency signals. During daylight hours, SSB and CW operation on 160 meters and 80 meters is confined to ground wave coverage. On 40 meters, daytime skip distances are generally no greater than 600 miles when the D layer is doing its thing absorbing MF and HF signals.

G3C06 What is a characteristic of HF scatter signals?

    A. High intelligibility
    B. A wavering sound
    C. Reversed modulation
    D. Reversed sidebands

ANSWER B: High frequency scatter communications bounce a portion of your signal off of densely ionized patches in the ionosphere. Since the ionosphere is constantly in motion, the signals will fade in and out, much like ocean waves.

G3C07 What makes HF scatter signals often sound distorted?

    A. Auroral activity and changes in the earth's magnetic field
    B. Propagation through ground waves that absorb much of the signal
    C. The state of the E-region at the point of refraction
    D. Energy scattered into the skip zone through several radio-wave paths

ANSWER D: The wavy sound of HF scatter signals, especially backscatter, is caused by the signal being reflected back through several radio-wave paths, creating multi-path distortion.

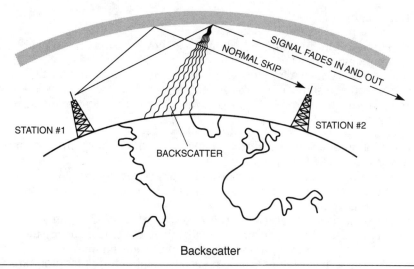

Backscatter

G3C08 Why are HF scatter signals usually weak?
 A. Only a small part of the signal energy is scattered into the skip zone
 B. Auroral activity absorbs most of the signal energy
 C. Propagation through ground waves absorbs most of the signal energy
 D. The F region of the ionosphere absorbs most of the signal energy
ANSWER A: During periods of scatter communications, only a fraction of the original signal is scattered back to those stations too far for ground-wave reception, yet too close for the main part of your signal being reflected by the ionosphere.

G3C09 What type of radio-wave propagation allows a signal to be detected at a distance too far for ground-wave propagation but too near for normal sky-wave propagation?
 A. Ground wave
 B. Scatter
 C. Sporadic-E skip
 D. Short-path skip
ANSWER B: Backscatter communications is one way to reach a station that is in that zone of no-reception—the skip zone. When your author communicates from Southern California to Seattle, San Francisco is in his skip zone and will not receive his signals. But if he aims his beam antenna west toward Hawaii, some of his signal is backscattered into the Bay Area, giving him communications to a station that is too far for ground wave, and too close for normal sky waves.

G3C10 When does scatter propagation on the HF bands most often occur?
- A. When the sunspot cycle is at a minimum and D-region absorption is high
- B. At night
- C. When the F1 and F2 regions are combined
- D. When communicating on frequencies above the maximum usable frequency (MUF)

ANSWER D: If you chose a frequency slightly above the maximum usable frequency, you can sometimes take advantage of the ionosphere to scatter your communications to an area that normally would not hear radio-wave reflection from the ionosphere.

G3C11 What is one way the vertical incidence critical frequency measurement might be used?
- A. It can be used to measure noise arriving vertically from outer space
- B. It can be used to measure the vertical angle at which to set your beam antenna
- C. It can be used to determine the size of coronal holes in the ionosphere
- D. It can be used to determine the maximum usable frequency for long-distance communication at the time of measurement

ANSWER D: There are some nifty propagation prediction computer programs available to determine the maximum usable frequency to a DX station. The computer programs take into account the vertical incidence critical frequency, which depends on where we are in the solar cycle, time of day, direction of the intended signal, A & K index, plus a host of other ionospheric variables. You can use the computer program to find out what might be the best time and the best band to work a long-range station.

Subelement G4 – Amateur Radio Practices (5 exam questions – 5 topic groups)

G4A Two-tone test; electronic TR switch; amplifier neutralization

G4A01 What kind of input signal is used to test the amplitude linearity of a single-sideband phone transmitter while viewing the output on an oscilloscope?
- A. Normal speech
- B. An audio-frequency sine wave
- C. Two audio-frequency sine waves
- D. An audio-frequency square wave

ANSWER C: We use two audio tones to test for proper linearity while viewing the tones on an oscilloscope. These pure tones, not harmonically related, will give you a stable picture on the scope if your transmitter amplifier has proper linearity.

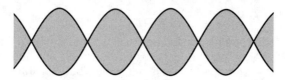

a. Properly Adjusted

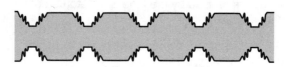

b. Distortion

Two-Tone Test

G4A02 When testing the amplitude linearity of a single-sideband transmitter, what kind of audio tones are fed into the microphone input and on what kind of instrument is the transmitter output observed?
  A. Two harmonically related tones are fed in, and the output is observed on an oscilloscope
  B. Two harmonically related tones are fed in, and the output is observed on a distortion analyzer
  C. Two non harmonically related tones are fed in, and the output is observed on an oscilloscope
  D. Two non harmonically related tones are fed in, and the output is observed on a distortion analyzer
ANSWER C: Many ham sets have an accessory "station monitor" oscilloscope that will allow you to check for proper modulation by looking at the waveform of the two tones fed into the mike circuit. Remember, key words are non-harmonically and oscilloscope.

G4A03 What audio frequencies are used in a two-tone test of the linearity of a single-sideband phone transmitter?
  A. 20 Hz and 20-kHz tones must be used
  B. 1200 Hz and 2400 Hz tones must be used
  C. Any two audio tones may be used, but they must be within the transmitter audio passband, and must be harmonically related
  D. Any two audio tones may be used, but they must be within the transmitter audio passband, and should not be harmonically related
ANSWER D: Adjust your two-tone generator so that the two audio tones are *not harmonically related,* and low enough in frequency to be passed through the transmitter audio circuitry.

G4A04 What measurement can be made of a single-sideband phone transmitter's amplifier by performing a two-tone test using an oscilloscope?
  A. Its percent of frequency modulation
  B. Its percent of carrier phase shift

C. Its frequency deviation

D. Its linearity

ANSWER D: The two-tone test, using an oscilloscope, is one of the best ways to check for SSB linearity. Another good way is to simply ask another station how you sound over the air. If the station is relatively close, tell them to turn off their noise blanker in order to hear your signal more clearly. Turning on a noise blanker will dramatically garble strong incoming signals at the receiver. Many a ham has given a fellow amateur operator a bad signal report when actually the signal was pure. This is caused by the inherent distortion of most noise blankers on strong signals.

G4A05 At what point in an HF transceiver block diagram would an electronic TR switch normally appear?

A. Between the transmitter and low-pass filter

B. Between the low-pass filter and antenna

C. At the antenna feed point

D. At the power supply feed point

ANSWER A: The modern high-frequency transceiver seldom uses big switching relays that were found in older sets. Squeeze the microphone a couple of times, and see whether or not you hear any relays clicking. If you don't, you have solid-state TR switching. The TR switch is placed between the transmitter and low-pass filter on the inside of your set.

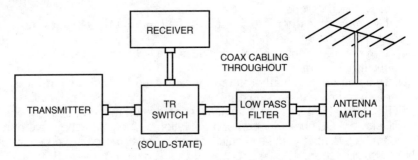

TR (Transmit/Receive) Switch Installation

G4A06 Why is an electronic TR switch preferable to a mechanical one?

A. It allows greater receiver sensitivity

B. Its circuitry is simpler

C. It has a higher operating speed

D. It allows cleaner output signals

ANSWER C: If you operate digital modes, such as packet or AMTOR, or if you operate high-speed, full break-in CW, the electronic TR circuit operates at a much higher speed than mechanical relays.

G4A07 As a power amplifier is tuned, what reading on its grid-current meter indicates the best neutralization?

A. A minimum change in grid current as the output circuit is changed

B. A maximum change in grid current as the output circuit is changed

C. Minimum grid current

D. Maximum grid current

ANSWER A: When the neutralizing capacitor is properly adjusted, there will be a minimum change on your grid current meter as you make small adjustments to the plate tank capacitor. It is the minimum *change* in grid current that indicates best neutralization, not necessarily minimum grid current.

G4A08 Why is neutralization necessary for some vacuum-tube amplifiers?
  A. To reduce the limits of loaded Q
  B. To reduce grid-to-cathode leakage
  C. To cancel AC hum from the filament transformer
  D. To cancel oscillation caused by the effects of interelectrode
     capacitance
ANSWER D: Most high-power, high-frequency Amateur Radio amplifiers use vacuum tubes for 1500 watts of maximum legal output power. Neutralization is sometimes necessary to cancel oscillation caused by the effects of interelectrode capacitance on the new tubes that you have just installed.

G4A09 In a properly neutralized RF amplifier, what type of feedback is used?
  A. 5%
  B. 10%
  C. Negative
  D. Positive
ANSWER C: When we neutralize an amplifier, we take a small amount of the output signal, shift it 180 degrees, and feed it back into the input. The feedback signal works against the input signal so it is called negative feedback.

G4A10 What does a neutralizing circuit do in an RF amplifier?
  A. It controls differential gain
  B. It cancels the effects of positive feedback
  C. It eliminates AC hum from the power supply
  D. It reduces incidental grid modulation
ANSWER B: Neutralization of an RF amplifier cancels the effects of positive feedback. When an amplifier goes into positive feedback, the grid current increases to a full deflection, the amplifier goes into oscillation, and unless you unkey the mike quickly, the output tube will go into meltdown in short order.

G4A11 What is the reason for neutralizing the final amplifier stage of a transmitter?
  A. To limit the modulation index
  B. To eliminate self oscillations
  C. To cut off the final amplifier during standby periods
  D. To keep the carrier on frequency
ANSWER B: After new tubes have been installed in a powerful amplifier, follow the instruction manual steps for neutralization, which will eliminate the possibility of self-oscillation.

G4B Test equipment: oscilloscope; signal tracer; antenna noise bridge; monitoring oscilloscope; field-strength meters

G4B01 What item of test equipment contains horizontal- and vertical-channel amplifiers?
    A. An ohmmeter
    B. A signal generator
    C. An ammeter
    D. An oscilloscope

ANSWER D: An oscilloscope is your best piece of test equipment if you are a technical amateur operator. But it takes skill to work a "scope," so don't buy one unless you know how to use it. The oscilloscope has horizontal- and vertical-channel amplifiers.

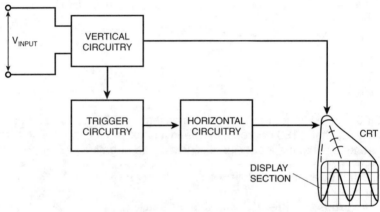

Simplified Diagram of an Oscilloscope

G4B02 What is a digital oscilloscope?
    A. An oscilloscope used only for signal tracing in digital circuits
    B. An oscilloscope used only for troubleshooting computers
    C. An oscilloscope used only for troubleshooting switching power supply circuits
    D. An oscilloscope designed around digital technology rather than analog technology

ANSWER D: Digital oscilloscopes look a bit like your portable LCD digital volt ohm meter. The digital technology allows for smaller, low-voltage components on the inside, plus an LCD screen to actually show wave forms. This is a big change from the old analog oscilloscopes that required high voltage to drive the green cathode ray display tube.

G4B03 How would a signal tracer normally be used?
    A. To identify the source of radio transmissions
    B. To make exact drawings of signal waveforms
    C. To show standing wave patterns on open-wire feed-lines
    D. To identify an inoperative stage in a receiver

ANSWER D: A signal tracer provides a source signal to the point in the circuit chosen by you. With normal receiver volume, you can usually hear the tone of the signal tracer coming through. Start at the speaker circuit, and work backwards, stage by stage, until the tone abruptly disappears. This will allow you to detect a stage that may have a problem.

G4B04 Why would you use a noise bridge?
A. To measure the noise figure of an antenna or other electrical circuit
B. To measure the impedance of an antenna or other electrical circuit
C. To cancel electrical noise picked up by an antenna
D. To tune out noise in a receiver

ANSWER B: An antenna noise bridge is an excellent accessory for checking out your new worldwide antenna system without actually running your radio power into it. It will allow you to calculate the antenna impedance by small adjustments to the bridge to see whether or not a mismatched antenna is simply too long, too short, or has problems with the feedpoint. These are portable devices and can literally save you hours in tracking down antenna problems.

Antenna Noise Bridge
Courtesy of MFJ Enterprises, Inc.

G4B05 How is a noise bridge normally used?
A. It is connected at an antenna's feed point and reads the antenna's noise figure
B. It is connected between a transmitter and an antenna and is tuned for minimum SWR
C. It is connected between a receiver and an antenna of unknown impedance and is tuned for minimum noise
D. It is connected between an antenna and ground and is tuned for minimum SWR

ANSWER C: You may use a noise bridge between your amateur receiver and an unknown impedance. Tune the antenna noise bridge for minimum noise and then read the impedance on the dial. Never transmit when this device is connected in the line.

G4B06 What is the best instrument to use to check the signal quality of a CW or single-sideband phone transmitter?
A. A monitoring oscilloscope
B. A field-strength meter
C. A sidetone monitor
D. A signal tracer and an audio amplifier

ANSWER A: The oscilloscope is your best instrument to check for signal quality. When magazine editors review the waveform of a CW signal or a two-tone test, they usually show photographs of the oscilloscope display.

G4B07 What signal source is connected to the vertical input of a monitoring oscilloscope when checking the quality of a transmitted signal?
A. The IF output of a monitoring receiver
B. The audio input of the transmitter
C. The RF signals of a nearby receiving antenna
D. The RF output of the transmitter

ANSWER D: We take the RF output of the transmitter and couple it to the vertical input of a monitoring oscilloscope to check the quality of the transmitted signal.

G4B08 What instrument can be used to determine the horizontal radiation pattern of an antenna?
A. A field-strength meter
B. A grid-dip meter
C. An oscilloscope
D. A signal tracer and an audio amplifier

ANSWER A: For antenna radiation pattern checks, use a field-strength meter. Place the field-strength meter several hundred feet away from the antenna and record the signal measurements. Keep your body away from the pick-up antenna on the field-strength meter because it could influence the reading.

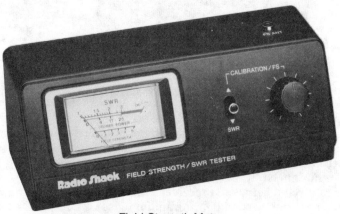

Field-Strength Meter

G4B09 How is a field-strength meter normally used?
A. To determine the standing-wave ratio on a transmission line
B. To check the output modulation of a transmitter
C. To monitor relative RF output
D. To increase average transmitter output

ANSWER C: A field-strength meter can only indicate relative output, not true power output.

G4B10 What simple instrument may be used to monitor relative RF output during antenna and transmitter adjustments?
A. A field-strength meter
B. An antenna noise bridge

C. A multimeter

D. A metronome

ANSWER A: For relative transmitter output checks, an inexpensive field-strength meter is a good addition to any ham station.

G4B11 By how many times must the power output of a transmitter be increased to raise the S-meter reading on a nearby receiver from S8 to S9?

A. Approximately 2 times

B. Approximately 3 times

C. Approximately 4 times

D. Approximately 5 times

ANSWER C: Seeing an S-meter change from S8 to S9 is an increase of a single S unit. One S unit is 6 dB and 6 dB is a 4 times change. Here is how the dB system for power works:

> 0 dB = 0 times change
> 3 dB = 2 times change
> 6 dB = 4 times change
> 9 dB = 8 times change
> 10 dB = 10 times change

G4C Audio rectification in consumer electronics; RF ground

G4C01 What devices would you install in home-entertainment systems to reduce or eliminate audio-frequency interference?

A. Bypass inductors

B. Bypass capacitors

C. Metal-oxide varistors

D. Bypass resistors

ANSWER B: When you begin operating on General Class frequencies, your powerful, high-frequency SSB transceiver fed into a roof antenna system will probably create audio-frequency interference to your own home electronics, and those of your surrounding four neighbors. Bypass capacitors—usually .01 µF—will sometimes help minimize this problem when strategically placed across and onto speaker wires and wiring harnesses inside the affected home electronic systems. It's not a cure-all—but bypass capacitors are your first step in resolving interference complaint problems on a case-by-case basis.

G4C02 What should be done if a properly operating amateur station is the cause of interference to a nearby telephone?

A. Make internal adjustments to the telephone equipment

B. Install RFI filters at the affected telephone

C. Stop transmitting whenever the telephone is in use

D. Ground and shield the local telephone distribution amplifier

ANSWER B: Telephone RFI (radio frequency interference) filters may need to be installed at the drop point where the phone lines enter the house. The phone company may install these filters at no charge; however, you will probably need to buy additional filters to be placed in series with the phone jack lines inside the house. Phone companies could also do this, but for a charge.

G4C03 What sound is heard from a public-address system if audio rectification of a nearby single-sideband phone transmission occurs?
   A. A steady hum whenever the transmitter's carrier is on the air
   B. On-and-off humming or clicking
   C. Distorted speech from the transmitter's signals
   D. Clearly audible speech from the transmitter's signals
ANSWER C: Single-sideband sounds like distorted speech coming over a public address system or certain home electronics. However, AM CB radio transmissions usually come through loud and clear, so these are easily distinguished from SSB ham transmissions. If someone says you are causing interference, ask the big question: "Does it sound garbled, or does it sound clear?"

G4C04 What sound is heard from a public-address system if audio rectification of a nearby CW transmission occurs?
   A. On-and-off humming or clicking
   B. Audible, possibly distorted speech
   C. Muffled, severely distorted speech
   D. A steady whistling
ANSWER A: CW transmissions come over a PA or home electronics system as on-and-off humming or clicking sounds. There is no mistaking the sound of CW.

G4C05 How can you minimize the possibility of audio rectification of your transmitter's signals?
   A. By using a solid-state transmitter
   B. By using CW emission only
   C. By ensuring that all station equipment is properly grounded
   D. By installing bypass capacitors on all power supply rectifiers
ANSWER C: Grounding your equipment to an earth-grounded copper pipe is one way to begin to minimize audio rectification interference. Turning down your power will help, too. Also, relocating your antenna far away from your neighbor's house will help. Finally, not transmitting during the Super Bowl would always be good advice.

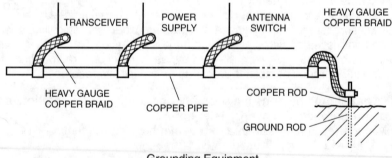

Grounding Equipment

G4C06 If your third-floor amateur station has a ground wire running 33 feet down to a ground rod, why might you get an RF burn if you touch the front panel of your HF transceiver?
   A. Because the ground rod is not making good contact with moist earth
   B. Because the transceiver's heat-sensing circuit is not working to start the cooling fan

C. Because of a bad antenna connection, allowing the RF energy to take an easier path out of the transceiver through you

D. Because the ground wire is a resonant length on several HF bands and acts more like an antenna than an RF ground connection

ANSWER D: A 33-foot ground wire becomes self-resonant on both 40 meters and 15 meters, giving you the chance of getting an RF burn as you hold the metal mike or touch the metal panel on your radio. Always use ground foil on long ground runs to minimize this problem.

G4C07 Which of the following is NOT an important reason to have a good station ground?

A. To reduce the cost of operating a station

B. To reduce electrical noise

C. To reduce interference

D. To reduce the possibility of electric shock

ANSWER A: A good earth ground on your home high-frequency station will give you a lower electrical noise floor, it will help reduce interference, and it will also reduce the possibility of an RF burn or electrical shock. However, a good ground won't necessarily reduce the cost of operating a station!

G4C08 What is one good way to avoid stray RF energy in your amateur station?

A. Keep the station's ground wire as short as possible

B. Use a beryllium ground wire for best conductivity

C. Drive the ground rod at least 14 feet into the ground

D. Make a couple of loops in the ground wire where it connects to your station

ANSWER A: If you run ground wires, as opposed to copper foil, keep those wires as short as possible.

G4C09 Which of the following statements about station grounding is NOT true?

A. Braid from RG-213 coaxial cable makes a good conductor to tie station equipment together into a station ground

B. Only transceivers and power amplifiers need to be tied into a station ground

C. According to the National Electrical Code, there should be only one grounding system in a building

D. The minimum length for a good ground rod is 8 feet

ANSWER B: Here is a question that asks for an answer that is not correct. ALL of your ham radio gear should be tied into a ground, not just the transceiver and power amp.

G4C10 Which of the following statements about station grounding is true?

A. The chassis of each piece of station equipment should be tied together with high-impedance conductors

B. If the chassis of all station equipment is connected with a good conductor, there is no need to tie them to an earth ground

C. RF hot spots can occur in a station located above the ground floor if the equipment is grounded by a long ground wire

D. A ground loop is an effective way to ground station equipment

---

ANSWER C: If you run a long ground wire, RF "hot spots" could occur in a ham station no matter where it is located inside the building. Keep your ground wire runs short.

G4C11 Which of the following is NOT covered in the National Electrical Code?
A. Minimum conductor sizes for different lengths of amateur antennas
B. The size and composition of grounding conductors
C. Electrical safety inside the ham shack
D. The RF exposure limits of the human body
ANSWER D: The National Electrical Code covers electrical safety standards as they relate to conductors. RF exposure limits to the human body are covered by ANSI, not by the NEC.

G4D Speech processors; PEP calculations; wire sizes and fuses

G4D01 What is the reason for using a properly adjusted speech processor with a single-sideband phone transmitter?
A. It reduces average transmitter power requirements
B. It reduces unwanted noise pickup from the microphone
C. It improves voice-frequency fidelity
D. It improves signal intelligibility at the receiver
ANSWER D: Properly adjusting your transmitter's speech processor will improve the intelligibility of your signal allowing it to be better heard at the receiving station.

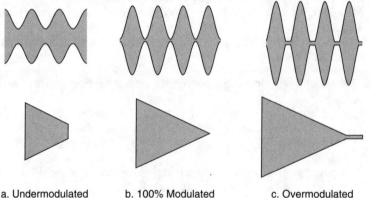

a. Undermodulated   b. 100% Modulated   c. Overmodulated

Speech Processor Waveforms

G4D02 If a single-sideband phone transmitter is 100% modulated, what will a speech processor do to the transmitter's power?
A. It will increase the output PEP
B. It will add nothing to the output PEP
C. It will decrease the peak power output
D. It will decrease the average power output
ANSWER B: Turning on your transceiver's speech processor will not increase PEP output power if you are 100 percent modulated. It will only increase the average power, and many times makes your signal sound "too hot" for comfort. Stay off that speech processor button unless it's absolutely necessary.

G4D03 How is the output PEP of a transmitter calculated if an oscilloscope is used to measure the transmitter's peak load voltage across a resistive load?
    A. PEP = [(Vp)(Vp)] / (RL)
    B. PEP = [(0.707 PEV)(0.707 PEV)] / RL
    C. PEP = (Vp)(Vp)(RL)
    D. PEP = [(1.414 PEV)(1.414 PEV)] / RL
ANSWER B: Peak envelope power is abbreviated PEP. Multiply 0.707 times peak envelope voltage (PEV), then multiply this quantity by itself—in other words, the PEV quantity times 0.707 is squared. Divide the squared quantity by the resistance of the load (RL). Look for an answer with a pair of "707's."

G4D04 What is the output PEP from a transmitter if an oscilloscope measures 200 volts peak-to-peak across a 50-ohm resistor connected to the transmitter output?
    A. 100 watts
    B. 200 watts
    C. 400 watts
    D. 1000 watts
ANSWER A: Let's use the equation given from the problem above:

$$PEP = (\text{peak voltage} \times 0.707)^2 \div \text{resistance of the load}$$

Watch out—the question reads 200 volts peak-to-peak. Peak voltage is one-half of the peak-to-peak value, or 100. Multiply 100×0.707 for 70.7. Multiply 70.7 by 70.7 to square the result for $(70.7)^2$ then divide by 50. Here are the calculator key strokes: Clear $100 \times 0.707 \times 70.7 \div 50 = 99.97$, which rounds off to 100 watts.

G4D05 What is the output PEP from a transmitter if an oscilloscope measures 500 volts peak-to-peak across a 50-ohm resistor connected to the transmitter output?
    A. 500 watts
    B. 625 watts
    C. 1250 watts
    D. 2500 watts
ANSWER B: Again take half the peak-to-peak voltage to obtain the peak voltage. Multiply 250×0.707, square the result (176.75) by multiplying by itself, and divide by 50. Here are the calculator key strokes: Clear $250 \times 0.707 \times 176.75 \div 50 = 624.81$, which rounds off to 625 watts.

G4D06 What is the output PEP of an unmodulated carrier transmitter if an average-reading wattmeter connected to the transmitter output indicates 1060 watts?
    A. 530 watts
    B. 1060 watts
    C. 1500 watts
    D. 2120 watts
ANSWER B: You won't need your calculator for this one. A transmitter with no modulation (unmodulated carrier) is putting out 1060 watts average, with all peaks at 1060 watts. Because of the steady unmodulated carrier, peak power and average power are the same.

G4D07 Which wires in a four-conductor line cord should be attached to fuses in a 240-VAC primary (single phase) power supply?
A. Only the "hot" (black and red) wires
B. Only the "neutral" (white) wire
C. Only the ground (bare) wire
D. All wires

ANSWER A: On 240-volt house power, the two hot wires are always fused. They are the red and black wires. The white wire is neutral and is never fused, and the green or bare ground wire also is never fused.

G4D08 What size wire is normally used on a 15-ampere, 120-VAC household lighting circuit?
A. AWG number 14
B. AWG number 16
C. AWG number 18
D. AWG number 22

ANSWER A: Number 14 wire can easily handle 15 amperes of current. Most home lamps have lamp cords using number 14 wire. Number 14 is rated at 17 amperes maximum in bundled wire cables.

Wire Size A.W.G. (B&S)	Current-Amps (Continuous Duty)	
	Single Wire	Bundled Wire
8	73	46
10	55	33
12	41	23
14	32	17
16	22	13
18	16	10

American Wire Gauge (AWG) Wire Size vs. Current Capability

G4D09 What size wire is normally used on a 20-ampere, 120-VAC household appliance circuit?
A. AWG number 20
B. AWG number 16
C. AWG number 14
D. AWG number 12

ANSWER D: Remember, the larger the wire, the smaller the AWG number. It takes a larger diameter, number 12, wire to handle up to 20 amperes of current on 120 volts AC. This is the wire size normally used on toasters and microwave ovens. Number 12 wire is rated at 23 amperes maximum in a bundled cable.

G4D10 What maximum size fuse or circuit breaker should be used in a household appliance circuit using AWG number 12 wiring?
A. 100 amperes
B. 60 amperes
C. 30 amperes
D. 20 amperes

ANSWER D: Since AWG number 12 wire can safely handle up to 20 amperes, you would normally fuse it for 20 amps.

G4D11 What maximum size fuse or circuit breaker should be used in a household appliance circuit using AWG number 14 wiring?
A. 15 amperes
B. 20 amperes
C. 30 amperes
D. 60 amperes
ANSWER A: A long 14-gauge wire will begin to get warm when more than 15 amperes pass through it. A 15-ampere fuse is the largest to use for safe operation.

G4E Common connectors used in amateur stations; types; when to use; fastening methods; precautions when using; HF mobile radio installations; emergency power systems; generators; battery storage devices and charging sources, including solar; wind generation

G4E01 Which of the following connectors is NOT designed for RF transmission lines?
A. PL-259
B. Type N
C. BNC
D. DB-25
ANSWER D: The DB-25 connector is designed for your computer. It is not a radio frequency transmission line connector. A PL-259 is sometimes called a "UHF" connector, and this is what goes to most worldwide HF transceivers. A Type N connector is what most 440 and 1270 transceivers use, and an BNC is what goes on top of most (but not all!) hand-helds. Some handhelds may also use a TNC connector, and the little micro-handhelds may now use an SMA connector. When you buy another handheld, doublecheck what type of antenna jack it has on the top.

BNC, Type N. and PL 259 Connectors

G4E02 When installing a power plug on a line cord, which of the following should you do?
A. Twist the wire strands neatly and fasten them so they don't cause a short circuit
B. Observe the correct wire color conventions for plug terminals

C. Use proper grounding techniques
D. All of these choices

ANSWER D: When you bring home that new kilowatt amplifier, chances are it will not have a power plug attached to the AC power line coming from the amp. This is a job that you get to do, but only after you have selected the right voltage for the amplifier—110 volts AC, or 220 volts AC. When you wire the plug, observe the correct wire color conventions for the plug terminals, twist the wire strands neatly and make sure there are no loose strands that could cause a short, and always use proper grounding techniques.

G4E03 Which of the following power connections would be the best for a 100-watt HF mobile installation?
A. A direct, fused connection to the battery using heavy gauge wire
B. A connection to the fuse-protected accessory terminal strip or distribution panel
C. A connection to the cigarette lighter
D. A direct connection to the alternator or generator

ANSWER A: As a General Class operator, you will probably be running a 100-watt, high-frequency, mobile transceiver in your car. You cannot rely on the car's 12-volt wiring to support the necessary 20-amp (minimum) power demands from your new radio. Wire your red and black power leads directly to the battery using heavy-gauge wire. Fuse both the red and the black power leads.

G4E04 Why is it best NOT to draw the DC power for a 100-watt HF transceiver from an automobile's cigarette lighter socket?
A. The socket is not wired with an RF-shielded power cable
B. The DC polarity of the socket is reversed from the polarity of modern HF transceivers
C. The power from the socket is never adequately filtered for HF transceiver operation
D. The socket's wiring may not be adequate for the current being drawn by the transceiver

ANSWER D: While you might be tempted to grab 12 volts from an automobile cigarette lighter socket, DON'T. Sure, the radio will work for a few minutes, but after a little bit of transmitting, the cigarette lighter receptacle wiring will get red hot, and quite possibly ignite more than what it was supposed to light up!

G4E05 Which of the following most limits the effectiveness of an HF mobile transceiver operating in the 75-meter band?
A. The vehicle's electrical system wiring
B. The wire gauge of the DC power line to the transceiver
C. The HF mobile antenna system
D. The rating of the vehicle's alternator or generator

ANSWER C: 75 meters is a great nighttime band for talking more than 1,000 miles away. However, to get on 75 meters with a mobile unit, you need a monster antenna loading coil and quite possibly a capacity hat on your antenna system. Your HF antenna system will be your biggest challenge when operating 75 meters, mobile.

G4E06 Which of the following is true of both a permanent or temporary emergency generator installation?

A. The generator should be located in a well ventilated area
B. The installation should be grounded
C. Extra fuel supplies, especially gasoline, should not be stored in an inhabited area
D. All of these choices

ANSWER D: When you set up for field day in June, chances are you may be using an emergency generator to keep all of the stations on the air. Make sure the generator is not located where some of the field day operators will inhale the toxic exhaust. Make sure the generator is properly grounded, and always store the generator's fuel in a safe place away from any inhabited area.

G4E07 Which of the following is true of a lead-acid storage battery as it is being charged?

A. It tends to cool off
B. It gives off explosive oxygen gas
C. It gives off explosive hydrogen gas
D. It takes in oxygen from the surrounding air

ANSWER C: Your author runs his home station off of a lead acid storage battery to keep him on the air in case of a blackout. The battery is outside because it gives off explosive hydrogen gas when it is being charged by solar panels, and it works very well. Never use a storage battery inside your ham shack because of the danger of explosive hydrogen gas.

G4E08 What is the name of the process by which sunlight is directly changed into electricity?

A. Photovoltaic conversion
B. Photosensitive conduction
C. Photosynthesis
D. Photocoupling

ANSWER A: You can change sunlight into VOLTAGE, and notice the word "volt" in the term photovoltaic conversion.

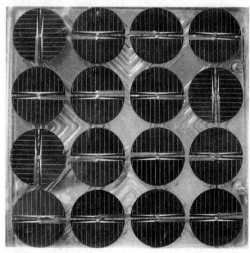

Close-up Photo of Solar Panel for Charging Storage Battery

G4E09 What is the approximate open-circuit voltage from a modern, well illuminated photovoltaic cell?

    A. 0.02 VDC

    B. 0.2 VDC

    C. 1.38 VDC

    D. 0.5 VDC

ANSWER D: A complete photovoltaic cell will yield 0.5 volts direct current. A solar panel is made up of a series-parallel connection of these cells in order to charge your storage battery system.

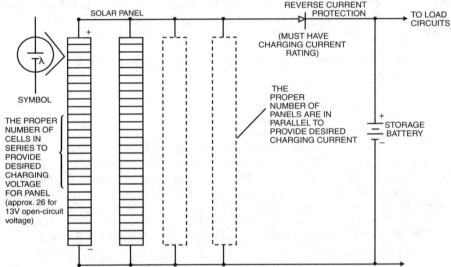

Schematic of Solar Panel for Charging Storage Battery

G4E10 What determines the proper size solar panel to use in a solar-powered battery-charging circuit?

    A. The panel's voltage rating and maximum output current

    B. The amount of voltage available per square inch of panel

    C. The panel's open-circuit current

    D. The panel's short-circuit voltage

ANSWER A: Most solar panels charge at a 12.8 volt DC level, but may have a much higher open-circuit voltage rating when measured without a battery connected. To determine the right solar panel for your system, check the panel's voltage rating and, most important, the maximum output current, usually expressed in amps if the panel is a relatively big one. The panel will have the necessary cells in series to provide the voltage, and the necessary voltage banks in parallel to supply the rated current. Expect to pay about $100 an ampere for a panel to charge a 12V battery.

G4E11 What is the biggest disadvantage to using wind power as the primary source of power for an emergency station?

    A. The conversion efficiency from mechanical energy to electrical energy is less that 2 percent

    B. The voltage and current ratings of such systems are not compatible with amateur equipment

C. A large electrical storage system is needed to supply power when the wind is not blowing

D. All of these choices are correct

ANSWER C: The wind doesn't blow all the time, so wind power is not a good primary source for your emergency communications station. When the wind isn't blowing, you need a huge bank of batteries to keep your station on the air.

Subelement G5 – Electrical Principles (2 exam questions – 2 topic groups)

G5A Impedance, including matching; resistance, including ohm; reactance, inductance, capacitance and metric divisions of these values

G5A01 What is impedance?
A. The electric charge stored by a capacitor
B. The opposition to the flow of AC in a circuit containing only capacitance
C. The opposition to the flow of AC in a circuit
D. The force of repulsion between one electric field and another with the same charge

ANSWER C: The term impedance means the opposition to the flow of alternating current in a circuit. Impedance to AC can be made up of resistance only, reactance only, or both resistance and reactance. You can create impedance to AC by winding a wire around a pencil to create a coil. This handy "choke" might minimize the alternator whine that may come in on your new worldwide mobile high-frequency station temporarily mounted in your vehicle.

G5A02 What is reactance?
A. Opposition to DC caused by resistors
B. Opposition to AC caused by inductors and capacitors
C. A property of ideal resistors in AC circuits
D. A large spark produced at switch contacts when an inductor is de-energized

ANSWER B: Inductive reactance is the opposition to AC caused by inductors. Capacitive reactance is the opposition to AC caused by capacitors. Both reactances vary with frequency. When there is an inductor and a capacitor in the same circuit, there is a special frequency, called the resonant frequency, where the inductive reactance equals the capacitive reactance.

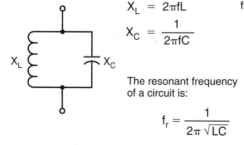

$$X_L = 2\pi fL$$

$$X_C = \frac{1}{2\pi fC}$$

The resonant frequency of a circuit is:

$$f_r = \frac{1}{2\pi \sqrt{LC}}$$

Resonant Frequency

The resonant frequency is the frequency where $X_L = X_C$.

$$\therefore 2\pi fL = \frac{1}{2\pi fC}$$

$$f^2 = \frac{1}{(2\pi L)(2\pi C)}$$

$$f^2 = \frac{1}{(2\pi)^2 LC}$$

$$\therefore f_r = \frac{1}{2\pi \sqrt{LC}}$$

G5A03 In an inductor, what causes opposition to the flow of AC?
A. Resistance
B. Reluctance
C. Admittance
D. Reactance

ANSWER D: Think of an inductor as a coil of wire. Its opposition to AC is called inductive reactance, identified as X_L. $X_L = 2\pi fL$ where f is the frequency in **hertz** and L is the inductance in **henries**. X_L increases as frequency increases.

G5A04 In a capacitor, what causes opposition to the flow of AC?
A. Resistance
B. Reluctance
C. Reactance
D. Admittance

ANSWER C: A capacitor has plates separated by an insulating dielectric. Its opposition to AC is called capacitive reactance, identified as X_C. $X_C = 1/2\pi fC$ where f is the frequency in **hertz** and C is the capacitance in **farads**. X_C decreases as frequency increases.

G5A05 How does a coil react to AC?
A. As the frequency of the applied AC increases, the reactance decreases
B. As the amplitude of the applied AC increases, the reactance increases
C. As the amplitude of the applied AC increases, the reactance decreases
D. As the frequency of the applied AC increases, the reactance increases

ANSWER D: Coils are effective in reducing alternator whine in high-frequency mobile installations. The higher the alternator whine frequency, the greater the reactance from the coil. Remember, as f increases, X_L increases ($X_L = 2\pi fL$).

G5A06 How does a capacitor react to AC?
A. As the frequency of the applied AC increases, the reactance decreases
B. As the frequency of the applied AC increases, the reactance increases
C. As the amplitude of the applied AC increases, the reactance increases
D. As the amplitude of the applied AC increases, the reactance decreases

ANSWER A: Capacitors offer reactance to AC inversely proportional to the frequency. Capacitors have high reactance at low frequencies and low reactance at high frequencies. Remember, as f increases, X_C decreases ($X_C = 1/2\pi fC$).

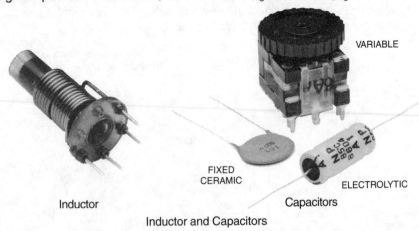

VARIABLE

FIXED
CERAMIC

ELECTROLYTIC

Inductor

Capacitors

Inductor and Capacitors

G5A07 When will a power source deliver maximum output to the load?
   A. When the impedance of the load is equal to the impedance of the source
   B. When the load resistance is infinite
   C. When the power-supply fuse rating equals the primary winding current
   D. When air wound transformers are used instead of iron-core transformers

ANSWER A: When we match the impedance of the load to the impedance of the source, we have the circuit conditions for maximum power transfer to the load. This is why it's important to ensure the antenna impedance matches that of your Amateur Radio transceiver. Most ham transceivers are rated for an impedance of 50 ohms.

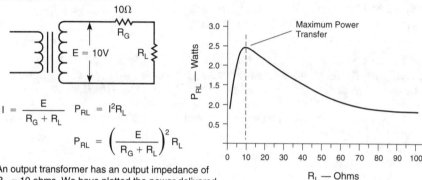

$$I = \frac{E}{R_G + R_L} \qquad P_{RL} = I^2 R_L$$

$$P_{RL} = \left(\frac{E}{R_G + R_L}\right)^2 R_L$$

An output transformer has an output impedance of $R_G = 10$ ohms. We have plotted the power delivered to R_L as R_L varies when $E = 10V$.
The values for the curve are calculated by substituting different values of R_L into the formula when $E = 10V$ and $R_G = 10\Omega$.
Maximum power is transferred when $R_G = R_L$.

Maximum Power Transfer

G5A08 What happens when the impedance of an electrical load is equal to the internal impedance of the power source?
   A. The source delivers minimum power to the load
   B. The electrical load is shorted
   C. No current can flow through the circuit
   D. The source delivers maximum power to the load

ANSWER D: Always make sure your new General Class worldwide antenna systems have an impedance around 50 ohms for maximum power transfer. Some General Class ham transceivers have built-in, automatic, impedance-matching antenna tuner networks.

G5A09 Why is impedance matching important?
   A. So the source can deliver maximum power to the load
   B. So the load will draw minimum power from the source
   C. To ensure that there is less resistance than reactance in the circuit
   D. To ensure that the resistance and reactance in the circuit are equal

ANSWER A: When internal source and load impedances are matched, maximum power will be delivered to the load.

G5A10 What unit is used to measure reactance?
A. Mho
B. Ohm
C. Ampere
D. Siemens

ANSWER B: The ohm is the unit of measurement for reactance as well as resistance.

G5A11 What unit is used to measure impedance?
A. Volt
B. Ohm
C. Ampere
D. Watt

ANSWER B: The ohm is also used for measuring impedance. Thus, the ohm may mean impedance, reactance, or resistance.

G5B Decibel; Ohm's law; current and voltage dividers; electrical power calculations and series and parallel components; transformers (either voltage or impedance); sine wave root-mean-square (RMS) value

G5B01 A two-times increase in power results in a change of how many dB?
A. 1 dB higher
B. 3 dB higher
C. 6 dB higher
D. 12 dB higher

ANSWER B: The decibel is used to describe a change in power levels. It is a measure of the ratio of power output to power input. A two-times increase results in a change of +3 dB.

If $dB = 10 \log_{10} \dfrac{P_1}{P_2}$

then what power ratio is 20 dB?

$20 = 10 \log_{10} \dfrac{P_1}{P_2}$

$\dfrac{20}{10} = \log_{10} \dfrac{P_1}{P_2}$

$2 = \log_{10} \dfrac{P_1}{P_2}$

Remember: logarithm of a number is the exponent to which the base must be raised to get the number.

$\therefore 10^2 = \dfrac{P_1}{P_2}$

$100 = \dfrac{P_1}{P_2}$

Or $P_1 = 100 \, P_2$

20 dB means P_1 is 100 times P_2

dB	$\dfrac{P_1}{P_2}$
3	2
6	4
10	10
20	100
30	1000
40	10000
50	10^5
60	10^6

Definition of a Decibel

Source: *The Technology Dictionary,* © 1987 Master Publishing, Inc., Lincolnwood, IL

G5B02 In a parallel circuit with a voltage source and several branch resistors, how is the total current related to the current in the branch resistors?
A. It equals the average of the branch current through each resistor
B. It equals the sum of the branch current through each resistor
C. It decreases as more parallel resistors are added to the circuit
D. It is the sum of each resistor's voltage drop multiplied by the total number of resistors

ANSWER B: If you add up the current in each branch resistance, you will come up with the total current in the circuit.

G5B03 How many watts of electrical power are used if 400 VDC is supplied to an 800-ohm load?
   A. 0.5 watts
   B. 200 watts
   C. 400 watts
   D. 320,000 watts
ANSWER B: The equation for this problem is $P = E^2 \div R$. 400^2 is 160,000. That divided by R (800) is 200, so the answer is 200 watts. Calculator keystrokes are: Clear, $400 \times 400 \div 800 = 200$.

G5B04 How many watts of electrical power are used by a 12-VDC light bulb that draws 0.2 amperes?
   A. 60 watts
   B. 24 watts
   C. 6 watts
   D. 2.4 watts
ANSWER D: Easy equation—power is equal to voltage times current ($P = E \times I$). Multiply volts times amps, and you end up with 2.4 watts. Using the magic circle below for voltage and current, put your finger over P, and find that power is equal to $E \times I$. Calculator keystrokes are: Clear, $12 \times .2 = 2.4$ (in watts).

P = POWER IN WATTS
E = VOLTAGE IN VOLTS
I = CURRENT IN AMPERES
R = RESISTANCE IN OHMS

Voltage and Current   Current and Resistance

Power Calculation

G5B05 How many watts are being dissipated when 7.0 milliamperes flow through 1.25 kilohms?
   A. Approximately 61 milliwatts
   B. Approximately 39 milliwatts
   C. Approximately 11 milliwatts
   D. Approximately 9 milliwatts
ANSWER A: Use the current and resistance version of the magic power circle above for the equation $P = I^2 \times R$. $I = 0.007$ amperes and $R = 1250$ ohms. Your answer will come out 0.061 watts. This is converted to 61 milliwatts by moving the decimal point 3 places to the right. Calculator keystrokes are: Clear, $.007 \times .007 \times 1250 = 0.06125$ (in watts).

G5B06 What is the voltage across a 500-turn secondary winding in a transformer if the 2250-turn primary is connected to 120 VAC?
   A. 2370 volts
   B. 540 volts
   C. 26.7 volts
   D. 5.9 volts

ANSWER C: This is a turns ratio problem, and is relatively easy to solve using the following equation:

$$E_S = E_P \times \frac{N_S}{N_P} = \frac{E_P \times N_S}{N_P}$$

which means the voltage of the secondary is equal to the voltage of the primary times the number of turns of the secondary divided by the number of turns of the primary. It is derived from the equation that says that the ratio of the secondary voltage, E_S, to the primary voltage, E_P, is equal to the ratio of the turns on the secondary, N_S, to the turns on the primary, N_P.

$$\frac{E_S}{E_P} = \frac{N_S}{N_P}$$

Multiply 120 (E_P) times 500 (N_S), and then divide your answer by 2250. This gives you 26.7 volts. Calculator keystrokes are: Clear, 120 × 500 ÷ 2250 =

G5B07 What is the turns ratio of a transformer to match an audio amplifier having a 600-ohm output impedance to a speaker having a 4-ohm impedance?
    A. 12.2 to 1
    B. 24.4 to 1
    C. 150 to 1
    D. 300 to 1

ANSWER A: The equation that applies is:

$$\frac{N_P}{N_S} = \sqrt{\frac{Z_P}{Z_S}} \qquad \text{derived from:} \qquad \frac{Z_P}{Z_S} = \left(\frac{I_S}{I_P}\right)^2 = \left(\frac{N_P}{N_S}\right)^2$$

The ratio of the turns on the *primary,* N_P, to the turns on the *secondary,* N_S, is equal to the square root of the ratio of the primary impedance, Z_P, to the secondary impedance, Z_S. Remember that this turns ratio is primary to secondary. The ratio in question G5B06 is secondary to primary.

    Don't worry if you have forgotten about square roots. There's an easy way to solve the problem. The primary impedance, Z_P, of the transformer must match the 600-ohms output impedance of the amplifier; therefore, Z_P is 600 ohms. Divide 600 ohms by 4 ohms, the speaker load impedance on the secondary, and you end up with 150.

    Now you need to find the square root of 150. You know that a square root multiplied by itself gives you the number you want. You can do it by approximation. Since 12 × 12 = 144 and 13 × 13 = 169, you know that the square root of 150 is between 12 and 13. The only answer given that is close is 12.2. Choose it and you have the correct answer. See, you didn't have to remember how to do square roots.

    The calculator keystrokes are: Clear, 600 ÷ 4 = 150, then press the square root key to produce the answer, 12.25.

G5B08 What is the impedance of a speaker that requires a transformer with a turns ratio of 24 to 1 to match an audio amplifier having an output impedance of 2000 ohms?
    A. 576 ohms
    B. 83.3 ohms

C. 7.0 ohms

D. 3.5 ohms

ANSWER D: Now you use the equation of question G5B07 a little differently. If you square the turns ratio N_P/N_S you get:

$$\left(\frac{N_P}{N_S}\right)^2 = \frac{Z_P}{Z_S} \text{ and } Z_S = \frac{Z_P}{T^2}$$

where T^2 is the square of primary to secondary turns ratio. The impedance of the secondary is equal to the impedance of the primary divided by the turns ratio squared. For this case:

$$Z_S = \frac{2000}{24^2} = \frac{2000}{576} = 3.47$$

As worked out, you see that you end up with about 3.5 ohms. Aren't most speakers around 3 or 4 ohms? Have you ever seen a speaker that has impedances like 576 ohms, or 83 ohms? Probably not—so you should immediately spot 3.5 ohms as the likely correct answer because that's what most speakers are! Maybe you didn't need to do all the calculations. Think it through! The oddball 7 ohms is temptingly close to 8 ohms, a common speaker impedance; so be careful of it.

G5B09 A DC voltage equal to what value of an applied sine-wave AC voltage would produce the same amount of heat over time in a resistive element?

A. The peak-to-peak value

B. The RMS value

C. The average value

D. The peak value

ANSWER B: The root mean square (RMS) voltage is the effective value of an ac voltage. The effective value of a sine wave voltage is the equivalent dc voltage value asked for in the question. To calculate peak value of a sine wave voltage, multiply the effective value by 1.414. To calculate the effective voltage from a peak voltage, multiply the peak voltage by 0.707.

$$E_{RMS} = 0.707\, E_{PK} \qquad\qquad E_{PP} = 2\, E_{PK}$$

$$E_{PK} = \frac{E_{RMS}}{0.707} \qquad\qquad E_{PK} = \frac{E_{PP}}{2}$$

$$E_{PK} = 1.414\, E_{RMS}$$

Basic AC Voltage Equations

G5B10 What is the peak-to-peak voltage of a sine wave that has an RMS voltage of 120 volts?

A. 84.8 volts

B. 169.7 volts

C. 204.8 volts

D. 339.4 volts

ANSWER D: First calculate the peak voltage of the 120 volts RMS by multiplying 120 times 1.414. Now multiply your answer by 2 since they are asking the peak-to-peak voltage! Watch out, this question asks peak-to-peak voltage, not just peak voltage. The calculator keystrokes are: Clear, 120 × 1.414 × 2 = 339.4.

G5B11 A sine wave of 17 volts peak is equivalent to how many volts RMS?
- A. 8.5 volts
- B. 12 volts
- C. 24 volts
- D. 34 volts

ANSWER B: Here we have an AC voltage of 17 volts peak. Multiply 17 times 0.707 to obtain the RMS voltage of 12 volts. Calculator keystrokes are: Clear, 17 × .707 = 12.02.

Subelement G6 – Circuit Components   (1 exam question – 1 topic group)

G6A Resistors; capacitors; inductors; rectifiers and transistors; etc.

G6A01 If a carbon resistor's temperature is increased, what will happen to the resistance?
- A. It will increase by 20% for every 10 degrees centigrade
- B. It will stay the same
- C. It will change depending on the resistor's temperature coefficient rating
- D. It will become time dependent

ANSWER C: Heating a carbon resistor always decreases its resistance. However, the amount of change for any particular temperature change depends on its temperature coefficient, which depends on the materials used in the resistor's construction.

G6A02 What type of capacitor is often used in power-supply circuits to filter the rectified AC?
- A. Disc ceramic
- B. Vacuum variable
- C. Mica
- D. Electrolytic

ANSWER D: Rectified AC is a form of pulsating DC. Electrolytic capacitors usually are used because they offer large amounts of capacity in a small size. The big problem with electrolytic capacitors—especially old ones—is that they dry out and lose their capacitance.

G6A03 What function does a capacitor serve if it is used in a power-supply circuit to filter transient voltage spikes across the transformer's secondary winding?
- A. Clipper capacitor
- B. Trimmer capacitor
- C. Feedback capacitor
- D. Suppressor capacitor

ANSWER D: If your new power supply suddenly fails after an obvious power surge at your home, check the suppressor capacitors for a short. These suppressor capacitors filter transient voltage spikes across the transformer's secondary winding.

G6A04 Where is the source of energy connected in a transformer?
    A. To the secondary winding
    B. To the primary winding
    C. To the core
    D. To the plates
ANSWER B: We hook up the energy source to a transformer's primary winding.

G6A05 If no load is attached to the secondary winding of a transformer, what is current in the primary winding called?
    A. Magnetizing current
    B. Direct current
    C. Excitation current
    D. Stabilizing current
ANSWER A: The load goes on the transformer's secondary. If there is no load, only the primary current necessary to develop the magnetic field in the primary will be present.

G6A06 What is the peak-inverse-voltage rating of a power-supply rectifier?
    A. The maximum transient voltage the rectifier will handle in the conducting direction
    B. 1.4 times the AC frequency
    C. The maximum voltage the rectifier will handle in the non-conducting direction
    D. 2.8 times the AC frequency
ANSWER C: The PIV rating of a power supply rectifier is the maximum voltage it will handle in the non-conducting direction.

G6A07 What are the two major ratings that must not be exceeded for silicon-diode rectifiers used in power-supply circuits?
    A. Peak inverse voltage; average forward current
    B. Average power; average voltage
    C. Capacitive reactance; avalanche voltage
    D. Peak load impedance; peak voltage
ANSWER A: Be sure to never exceed the peak-inverse-voltage rating and the average forward current rating of silicon-diode rectifiers used in power supplies.

G6A08 What is the output waveform of an unfiltered full-wave rectifier connected to a resistive load?
    A. A series of pulses at twice the frequency of the AC input
    B. A series of pulses at the same frequency as the AC input
    C. A sine wave at half the frequency of the AC input
    D. A steady DC voltage
ANSWER A: A full-wave rectifier gives a much smoother pulsating DC to filter than a half-wave rectifier because the full-wave rectified half sine waves are double the line frequency.

G6A09 A half-wave rectifier conducts during how many degrees of each cycle?
    A. 90 degrees
    B. 180 degrees
    C. 270 degrees
    D. 360 degrees
ANSWER B: The half-wave rectifier uses only half of the cycle, which is 180 degrees.

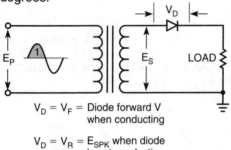

$V_D = V_F$ = Diode forward V when conducting

$V_D = V_R = E_{SPK}$ when diode is not conducting

Conducts only on positive cycle. No conduction on negative cycle.

Reverse voltage across diode is E_{SPK}, the peak voltage of the secondary voltage.

Half-Wave Rectifier

G6A10 A full-wave rectifier conducts during how many degrees of each cycle?
    A. 90 degrees
    B. 180 degrees
    C. 270 degrees
    D. 360 degrees
ANSWER D: A full-wave rectifier is much more efficient because it uses all 360 degrees. A full-wave rectifier output also is much easier to filter to provide pure DC voltage. See figure at question G7A01.

G6A11 When two or more diodes are connected in parallel to increase the current-handling capacity of a power supply, what is the purpose of the resistor connected in series with each diode?
    A. The resistors ensure that one diode doesn't take most of the current
    B. The resistors ensure the thermal stability of the power supply
    C. The resistors regulate the power supply output voltage
    D. The resistors act as swamping resistors in the circuit
ANSWER A: If you apply too much power to drive that new high-frequency kilowatt amplifier for General Class operation, you may overload the power supply, wiping out a diode or two. Over-driving the amp may also smoke some of those equalizing resistors. The resistors connected in series with each diode help ensure that one diode doesn't take most of the current. It's a good idea to keep the schematic diagrams of your new General Class station equipment handy in case you smoke something so badly you can't even read what the value was!

Subelement G7 – Practical Circuits   (1 exam question – 1 topic group)

G7A Power supplies and filters; single-sideband transmitters and receivers

G7A01 What safety feature does a power-supply bleeder resistor provide?
A. It improves voltage regulation
B. It discharges the filter capacitors
C. It removes shock hazards from the induction coils
D. It eliminates ground-loop current
ANSWER B: When you turn off your big rig, it dims down and then cycles off completely. This slow decay of voltage is from the filter capacitors that are slowly being discharged by the bleeder resistors. This is a safety feature, and also helps provide voltage regulation.

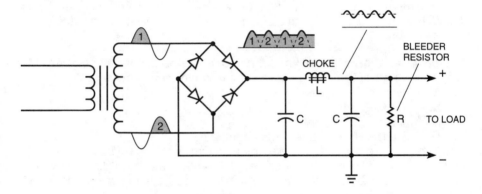

Full-Wave Power Supply with Bleeder Resistor

G7A02 Where is a power-supply bleeder resistor connected?
A. Across the filter capacitor
B. Across the power-supply input
C. Between the transformer primary and secondary windings
D. Across the inductor in the output filter
ANSWER A: The bleeder resistor is connected across the filter capacitor. See figure at previous question.

G7A03 What components are used in a power-supply filter network?
A. Diodes
B. Transformers and transistors
C. Quartz crystals
D. Capacitors and inductors
ANSWER D: In power supplies, transformers supply the voltage and current, diodes rectify, and capacitors and inductors filter. A bleeder resistor protects.

G7A04 What should be the minimum peak-inverse-voltage rating of the rectifier in a full-wave power supply?
A. One-quarter the normal output voltage of the power supply
B. Half the normal output voltage of the power supply

C. Equal to the normal output voltage of the power supply

D. Double the normal peak output voltage of the power supply

ANSWER D: Double or nothing! The peak-inverse-voltage rating of rectifier diodes normally is double for a full-wave power supply. This is because the diode is seeing the entire secondary winding, as opposed to just half of the secondary winding in the opposite direction. It's always a good idea to double the voltage rating of any type of capacitor or diode going into a power supply circuit.

G7A05 What should be the minimum peak-inverse-voltage rating of the rectifier in a half-wave power supply?

A. One-quarter to one-half the normal peak output voltage of the power supply

B. Half the normal output voltage of the power supply

C. Equal to the normal output voltage of the power supply

D. One to two times the normal peak output voltage of the power supply

ANSWER D: At least one time, but to be much more reliable, two times the peak voltage output.

G7A06 What should be the impedance of a low-pass filter as compared to the impedance of the transmission line into which it is inserted?

A. Substantially higher

B. About the same

C. Substantially lower

D. Twice the transmission line impedance

ANSWER B: As we discussed earlier, impedances should always be the same for maximum transfer of power. Therefore, you want the low-pass filter to have the same impedance as both the transmission line and the ham transceiver to which it is connected.

G7A07 In a typical single-sideband phone transmitter, what circuit processes signals from the balanced modulator and sends signals to the mixer?

A. Carrier oscillator

B. Filter

C. IF amplifier

D. RF amplifier

ANSWER B: In a typical SSB transceiver, it is the filter circuit that processes signals from the balanced modulator and sends them to the mixer.

G7A08 In a single-sideband phone transmitter, what circuit processes signals from the carrier oscillator and the speech amplifier and sends signals to the filter?

A. Mixer

B. Detector

C. IF amplifier

D. Balanced modulator

ANSWER D: In an SSB transceiver, the balanced modulator processes the signal from the carrier oscillator and the speech amplifier and sends it on to the filter.

G7A09 In a single-sideband phone superheterodyne receiver, what circuit processes signals from the RF amplifier and the local oscillator and sends signals to the IF filter?
A. Balanced modulator
B. IF amplifier
C. Mixer
D. Detector
ANSWER C: In an SSB receiver section, it is the mixer that processes signals from the RF amplifier and the local oscillator.

G7A10 In a single-sideband phone superheterodyne receiver, what circuit processes signals from the IF amplifier and the BFO and sends signals to the AF amplifier?
A. RF oscillator
B. IF filter
C. Balanced modulator
D. Detector
ANSWER D: In an SSB receiver, it is the detector that processes the signals from the IF amplifier and the BFO. The signal then goes to the audio frequency amplifier.

G7A11 In a single-sideband phone superheterodyne receiver, what circuit processes signals from the IF filter and sends signals to the detector?
A. RF oscillator
B. IF amplifier
C. Mixer
D. BFO
ANSWER B: In your worldwide SSB receiver, it is the job of the IF amplifier to process the signal from the IF filter and send it on to the detector.

Subelement G8 – Signals and Emissions   (2 exam questions – 2 topic groups)

G8A Signal information; AM; FM; single and double sideband and carrier; bandwidth; modulation envelope; deviation; overmodulation

G8A01 What type of modulation system changes the amplitude of an RF wave for the purpose of conveying information?
A. Frequency modulation
B. Phase modulation
C. Amplitude-rectification modulation
D. Amplitude modulation
ANSWER D: A type of modulation that will change the *AMPLITUDE* of an RF wave is called *amplitude modulation* (AM).

G8A02 What type of modulation system changes the phase of an RF wave for the purpose of conveying information?
A. Pulse modulation
B. Phase modulation
C. Phase-rectification modulation
D. Amplitude modulation

ANSWER B: A type of modulation that changes the **PHASE** of an RF wave is called *phase modulation* (PM).

G8A03 What type of modulation system changes the frequency of an RF wave for the purpose of conveying information?
    A. Phase-rectification modulation
    B. Frequency-rectification modulation
    C. Amplitude modulation
    D. Frequency modulation
ANSWER D: A type of modulation that changes the **FREQUENCY** of an RF wave is called *frequency modulation* (FM).

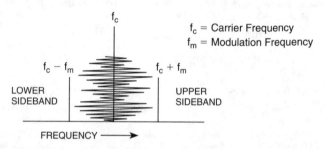

f_c = Carrier Frequency
f_m = Modulation Frequency

LOWER SIDEBAND $f_c - f_m$ f_c $f_c + f_m$ UPPER SIDEBAND

FREQUENCY ⟶

Carrier and Sidebands of an A3E Emission
(See Appendix, page 129, for explanation of Emission Type Designators.)

G8A04 What emission is produced by a reactance modulator connected to an RF power amplifier?
    A. Multiplex modulation
    B. Phase modulation
    C. Amplitude modulation
    D. Pulse modulation
ANSWER B: A reactance modulator produces *phase modulation,* which is used for phase modulation and frequency modulation.

G8A05 In what emission type does the instantaneous amplitude (envelope) of the RF signal vary in accordance with the modulating audio?
    A. Frequency shift keying
    B. Pulse modulation
    C. Frequency modulation
    D. Amplitude modulation
ANSWER D: The instantaneous **AMPLITUDE** of the signal varies with *amplitude modulation.*

G8A06 How much should the carrier be suppressed below peak output power in a properly designed single-sideband (SSB) transmitter?
    A. No more than 20 dB
    B. No more than 30 dB
    C. At least 40 dB
    D. At least 60 dB
ANSWER C: Life begins at 40. Carrier suppression of a single-sideband transmission is greater than 40 dB below the output power.

G8A07 What is one advantage of carrier suppression in a double-side-band phone transmission?
A. Only half the bandwidth is required for the same information content
B. Greater modulation percentage is obtainable with lower distortion
C. More power can be put into the sidebands
D. Simpler equipment can be used to receive a double-sideband sup-pressed-carrier signal

ANSWER C: SSB (single sideband) is more efficient than DSB (double sideband) because there is no power wasted in the carrier, nor is any power wasted in one of the unnecessary sidebands.

G8A08 Which popular phone emission uses the narrowest frequency bandwidth?
A. Single-sideband
B. Double-sideband
C. Phase-modulated
D. Frequency-modulated

ANSWER A: Single sideband is more efficient than most other types of voice communications because it occupies only 3 kHz of bandwidth.

G8A09 What happens to the signal of an overmodulated single-sideband or double-sideband phone transmitter?
A. It becomes louder with no other effects
B. It occupies less bandwidth with poor high-frequency response
C. It has higher fidelity and improved signal-to-noise ratio
D. It becomes distorted and occupies more bandwidth

ANSWER D: If you turn your transceiver's microphone gain too high, or engage the speech processor and turn it up too high, your signal will become distorted and will occupy more bandwidth.

G8A10 How should the microphone gain control be adjusted on a single-sideband phone transmitter?
A. For full deflection of the ALC meter on modulation peaks
B. For slight movement of the ALC meter on modulation peaks
C. For 100% frequency deviation on modulation peaks
D. For a dip in plate current

ANSWER B: Your author normally runs his microphone gain control on the SSB transceiver straight up and down in the 12:00 o'clock position. This allows a slight movement of the ALC meter on modulation peaks. As long as the meter stays within the ALC region marked on the meter, everything is fine.

G8A11 What is meant by flattopping in a single-sideband phone transmission?
A. Signal distortion caused by insufficient collector current
B. The transmitter's automatic level control is properly adjusted
C. Signal distortion caused by excessive drive
D. The transmitter's carrier is properly suppressed

ANSWER C: If you turn the microphone gain too high on SSB, that brand new rig will sound distorted. The signal waveform shown on an oscilloscope has the top clipped off so it has a flat top.

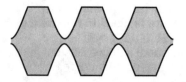

Oscilloscope Waveform Showing "Flattopping"

G8B Frequency mixing; multiplication; bandwidths; HF data communications

G8B01 What receiver stage combines a 14.25-MHz input signal with a 13.795-MHz oscillator signal to produce a 455-kHz intermediate frequency (IF) signal?
A. Mixer
B. BFO
C. VFO
D. Multiplier

ANSWER A: When you see that word "combines," think of the mixer section of a receiver stage.

G8B02 If a receiver mixes a 13.800-MHz VFO with a 14.255-MHz received signal to produce a 455-kHz intermediate frequency (IF) signal, what type of interference will a 13.345-MHz signal produce in the receiver?
A. Local oscillator
B. Image response
C. Mixer interference
D. Intermediate interference

ANSWER B: In strong signal areas where there may be local transmissions coming in from shortwave stations outside of normal ham band limits, an interference called "image response" may develop at the sum and difference of your intermediate frequency (IF) signal. 13.800 MHz minus 455 kHz is 13.345 MHz.

G8B03 What stage in a transmitter would change a 5.3-MHz input signal to 14.3 MHz?
A. A mixer
B. A beat frequency oscillator
C. A frequency multiplier
D. A linear translator

ANSWER A: It's the job of the mixer to change a 5.3 MHz input signal up to 14.3 MHz by mixing in an oscillator frequency.

G8B04 What is the name of the stage in a VHF FM transmitter that selects a harmonic of an HF signal to reach the desired operating frequency?
A. Mixer
B. Reactance modulator
C. Preemphasis network
D. Multiplier
ANSWER D: Inside a VHF FM transmitter is a low-power oscillator that operates at HF levels. It's the job of the multiplier to select a harmonic of this signal to produce the desired operating frequency.

G8B05 Why isn't frequency modulated (FM) phone used below 29.5 MHz?
A. The transmitter efficiency for this mode is low
B. Harmonics could not be attenuated to practical levels
C. The bandwidth would exceed FCC limits
D. The frequency stability would not be adequate
ANSWER C: We cannot use frequency modulation phone below 29.5 MHz because the bandwidth is simply too wide. Most FM simplex operation is found on 29.6 MHz, a good spot to enjoy your new General Class privileges. There are also repeaters up in this range.

G8B06 What is the total bandwidth of an FM-phone transmission having a 5-kHz deviation and a 3-kHz modulating frequency?
A. 3 kHz
B. 5 kHz
C. 8 kHz
D. 16 kHz
ANSWER D: You can calculate this answer by multiplying 2 times the sum of the deviation and highest audio modulating frequency. The deviation is 5 kHz plus 3 kHz of audio, which gives a sum of 8 kHz. Two times 8 kHz equals 16 kHz. This would be the total bandwidth of the FM phone transmission.

G8B07 What is the frequency deviation for a 12.21-MHz reactance-modulated oscillator in a 5-kHz deviation, 146.52-MHz FM-phone transmitter?
A. 41.67 Hz
B. 416.7 Hz
C. 5 kHz
D. 12 kHz
ANSWER B: This is an easy ratio problem. First, let's determine the frequency multiplication factor of the transmitter. Divide the 12.21 oscillator frequency into the output at 146.52. This gives us a multiplication factor of 12. If there is 5 kHz deviation at the transmitter, 1/12 deviation at the oscillator input is 12 divided into 5000 Hz, with an answer of 416.66 Hz.

G8B08 How is frequency shift related to keying speed in an FSK signal?
A. The frequency shift in hertz must be at least four times the keying speed in WPM
B. The frequency shift must not exceed 15 Hz per WPM of keying speed
C. Greater keying speeds require greater frequency shifts
D. Greater keying speeds require smaller frequency shifts

ANSWER C: The faster digital and code emissions are sent, the greater the bandwidth these emissions occupy.

Spacing	Mark	Space
170 Hz	2125 Hz	2295 Hz
170 Hz	1275 Hz	1445 Hz
200 Hz	1270 Hz	1070 Hz Originate
200 Hz	2225 Hz	2025 Hz Answer
425 Hz	2125 Hz	2550 Hz
850 Hz	2975 Hz	2125 Hz
850 Hz	1275 Hz*	2125 Hz

*British Standard, all others U. S. Standard.

Mark and Space Frequencies for FSK Spacing

Source: *Digital Communications with Packet Radio,* © 1988 Master Publishing, Inc., Lincolnwood, IL

G8B09 What do RTTY, Morse code, AMTOR and packet communications have in common?
 A. They are multipath communications
 B. They are digital communications
 C. They are analog communications
 D. They are only for emergency communications
ANSWER B: RTTY, Morse code, AMTOR, and packet are all forms of digital communication. Laptop computers with a small analog-to-digital converter, along with the right software, can easily decode these digital communications. Do you have a spare laptop you want to press into service on your new General Class bands?

G8B10 What is the duty cycle required of a transmitter when sending Mode B (FEC) AMTOR?
 A. 50%
 B. 75%
 C. 100%
 D. 125%
ANSWER C: When transmitting forward error correction (FEC) AMTOR, your transmitter must have a 100 percent duty cycle to keep it from overheating. An external fan wouldn't hurt, either!

G8B11 In what segment of the 20-meter band are most AMTOR operations found?
 A. At the bottom of the slow-scan TV segment, near 14.230 MHz
 B. At the top of the SSB phone segment, near 14.325 MHz
 C. In the middle of the CW segment, near 14.100 MHz
 D. At the bottom of the RTTY segment, near 14.075 MHz
ANSWER D: You will find most AMTOR operations just below the RTTY segment of the 20-meter band, near 14.075 MHz.

Subelement G9 – Antennas and Feed-Lines   (4 exam questions – 4 topic groups)

G9A Yagi antennas - physical dimensions; impedance matching; radiation patterns; directivity and major lobes

G9A01 How can the SWR bandwidth of a parasitic beam antenna be increased?
A. Use larger diameter elements
B. Use closer element spacing
C. Use traps on the elements
D. Use tapered-diameter elements
ANSWER A: The greater the diameter of the elements, the greater the bandwidth of a beam antenna for worldwide operation. This is why a wire beam antenna does not offer as much bandwidth as one constructed of large aluminum tubes.

G9A02 Approximately how long is the driven element of a Yagi antenna for 14.0 MHz?
A. 17 feet
B. 33 feet
C. 35 feet
D. 66 feet
ANSWER B: To calculate the length of the driven element of a Yagi antenna end-to-end for 14.0 MHz, use the following formula for a half-wave antenna (in feet):

$$\text{Driven element (in feet)} = \frac{\lambda}{2} = \frac{472}{f} \quad \text{where: } \lambda = \text{wavelength in feet}$$
$$f = \text{frequency in MHz}$$

The factor 472 divided by the frequency in MHz gives the length in feet of the driven element. No further division is necessary because the equation is for the entire length of the half-wave driven element. The calculator keystrokes are: Clear, 472 ÷ 14 = 33.71. (See page 124 for antenna equations.)

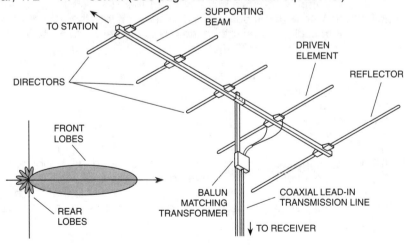

a. Directional Pattern   b. Physical Construction

A Beam Antenna - The Yagi Antenna

Source: *Antennas - Selection and Installation,* © 1986 Master Publishing, Inc., Lincolnwood, IL

G9A03 Approximately how long is the director element of a Yagi antenna for 21.1 MHz?
    A. 42 feet
    B. 21 feet
    C. 17 feet
    D. 10.5 feet
ANSWER B: Because the director needs to be shorter, the formula changes to:

$$\text{Director element (in feet)} = \frac{\lambda}{2} = \frac{458}{f} \quad \text{where: } \lambda = \text{wavelength in feet}$$
$$f = \text{frequency in MHz}$$

Use the factor 458 instead of 472, divided by the frequency in MHz to arrive at the length in feet of a director. Calculator keystrokes are: Clear, 458 ÷ 21.1 = 21.70.

G9A04 Approximately how long is the reflector element of a Yagi antenna for 28.1 MHz?
    A. 8.75 feet
    B. 16.6 feet
    C. 17.5 feet
    D. 35 feet
ANSWER C: Because the reflector must be a little bit longer, the formula changes to:

$$\text{Reflector element (in feet)} = \frac{\lambda}{2} = \frac{490}{f} \quad \text{where: } \lambda = \text{wavelength in feet}$$
$$f = \text{frequency in MHz}$$

The equation factor is 490, and is divided by the frequency in MHz for the length in feet of a reflector. The calculator keystrokes are: Clear, 490 ÷ 28.1 = 17.44.

G9A05 Which statement about a three-element Yagi antenna is true?
    A. The reflector is normally the shortest parasitic element
    B. The director is normally the shortest parasitic element
    C. The driven element is the longest parasitic element
    D. Low feed-point impedance increases bandwidth
ANSWER B: On a three-element beam, the director is shorter than the driven element, and the reflector is longer than the driven element. Study the Yagi antenna illustration at question G9A02.

G9A06 What is one effect of increasing the boom length and adding directors to a Yagi antenna?
    A. Gain increases
    B. SWR increases
    C. Weight decreases
    D. Wind load decreases
ANSWER A: On a worldwide (as well as VHF/UHF) Yagi antenna, boom length determines the amount of gain. The number of elements and the diameter of the elements influence the directivity and bandwidth of the antenna, but the big factor that determines which Yagi antenna is going to outperform another Yagi in gain is boom length.

G9A07 Why is a Yagi antenna often used for radio communications on the 20-meter band?
   A. It provides excellent omnidirectional coverage in the horizontal plane
   B. It is smaller, less expensive and easier to erect than a dipole or vertical antenna
   C. It helps reduce interference from other stations off to the side or behind
   D. It provides the highest possible angle of radiation for the HF bands

ANSWER C: When you pass your General Class license, the Yagi antenna will give you one of the best signals ever on the 20-meter band because it reduces interference from other stations off to the side or behind. A small, three-element Yagi works quite nicely just a few feet off the top of your house.

G9A08 What does "antenna front-to-back ratio" mean in reference to a Yagi antenna?
   A. The number of directors versus the number of reflectors
   B. The relative position of the driven element with respect to the reflectors and directors
   C. The power radiated in the major radiation lobe compared to the power radiated in exactly the opposite direction
   D. The power radiated in the major radiation lobe compared to the power radiated 90 degrees away from that direction

ANSWER C: The Yagi antenna gives you an excellent front-to-back ratio. This means that the majority of the power is radiated out of the front of the antenna, with little signal wasted to the back or to the sides. See illustration at G9A02.

G9A09 What is the "main lobe" of a Yagi antenna radiation pattern?
   A. The direction of least radiation from the antenna
   B. The point of maximum current in a radiating antenna element
   C. The direction of maximum radiated field strength from the antenna
   D. The maximum voltage standing wave point on a radiating element

ANSWER C: The main lobe is the main radiating direction of the signal. You may use a field strength meter to determine the main lobe of most Yagi antennas. See illustration at G9A02.

G9A10 What is a good way to get maximum performance from a Yagi antenna?
   A. Optimize the lengths and spacing of the elements
   B. Use RG-58 feed-line
   C. Use a reactance bridge to measure the antenna performance from each direction around the antenna
   D. Avoid using towers higher than 30 feet above the ground

ANSWER A: Choose your worldwide Yagi antenna carefully. Select one that has optimized lengths and spacing of the elements.

G9A11 Which of the following is NOT a Yagi antenna design variable that should be considered to optimize the forward gain, front-to-rear gain ratio and SWR bandwidth?
   A. The physical length of the boom
   B. The number of elements on the boom

C. The spacing of each element along the boom

D. The polarization of the antenna elements

ANSWER D: The physical length of the boom is the largest factor in determining forward gain of a Yagi antenna. The number of elements and the spacing of each element will influence the front-to-back ratio and SWR. However, polarization of the antenna elements on a Yagi antenna has no meaning when it comes to more or less gain.

G9B Loop antennas—physical dimensions; impedance matching; radiation patterns; directivity and major lobes

G9B01 Approximately how long is each side of a cubical-quad antenna driven element for 21.4 MHz?

A. 1.17 feet

B. 11.7 feet

C. 47 feet

D. 469 feet

ANSWER B: The cubical-quad antenna is a full-wavelength, four-sided, wire antenna system that offers identical to slightly improved performance over a Yagi. To determine the length of wire for each side of the driven element, use the following formula:

$$\text{Driven Element for each side (in feet)} = \frac{1005}{f \text{ (MHz)}} \div 4$$

First divide 21.4 MHz into 1005, and then divide your answer by 4 because they only want one side. The factor 1005 is used for the driven element only. Your answer, 11.74, is in feet. Calculator keystrokes are: Clear, 1005 ÷ 21.4 ÷ 4 = 11.74. (See page 124 for antenna equations.)

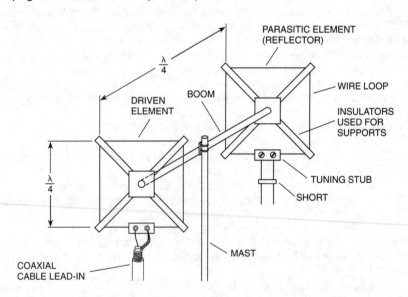

A Two-Element Cubical Quad Antenna - Horizontally Polarized

Source: *Antennas - Selection and Installation,* © 1986 Master Publishing, Inc., Lincolnwood, IL

G9B02 Approximately how long is each side of a cubical-quad antenna driven element for 14.3 MHz?
  A. 17.6 feet
  B. 23.4 feet
  C. 70.3 feet
  D. 175 feet

ANSWER A: Use the formula from the previous question. Divide the frequency 14.3 into 1005 to come up with 70.28 feet. Now divide this by 4 to calculate one side (17.6 feet) of the cubical-quad antenna used for working the 20 meter band.

G9B03 Approximately how long is each side of a cubical-quad antenna reflector element for 29.6 MHz?
  A. 8.23 feet
  B. 8.7 feet
  C. 9.7 feet
  D. 34.8 feet

ANSWER B: Here we need to calculate each side of the reflector element, which is always going to be a bit longer. Use the same formula as for the previous question but substitute 1030 for 1005, then divide by the frequency in MHz. Remember, divide your answer by 4 because they only want to know the dimension of one side. The calculator keystrokes are: Clear, 1030 ÷ 29.6 = 34.79 ÷ 4 = 8.7. The answer is in feet.

G9B04 Approximately how long is each leg of a symmetrical delta-loop antenna driven element for 28.7 MHz?
  A. 8.75 feet
  B. 11.7 feet
  C. 23.4 feet
  D. 35 feet

ANSWER B: The Delta-loop is another version of a full wavelength antenna system. The beauty of the delta-loop is you can put the apex of the loop way up at the top of a tree. Use the formula:

$$\text{Driven Element for each side (in feet)} = \frac{1005}{f \text{ (MHz)}} \div 3$$

Just as you did for the quad, divide 1005 by the frequency in MHz. However, since this is a delta-loop, and they only want to know one side, divide your answer by 3 instead of 4. Here are your calculator keystrokes: Clear, 1005 ÷ 28.7 = 35.02 ÷ 3 = 11.67.

G9B05 Approximately how long is each leg of a symmetrical delta-loop antenna driven element for 24.9 MHz?
  A. 10.99 feet
  B. 12.95 feet
  C. 13.45 feet
  D. 40.36 feet

ANSWER C: Use the same formula as in the previous question, and don't forget to divide by 3. A wrong answer is waiting for you if you don't. Calculator key-strokes are: Clear, 1005 ÷ 24.9 = 40.36 ÷ 3 = 13.45 feet.

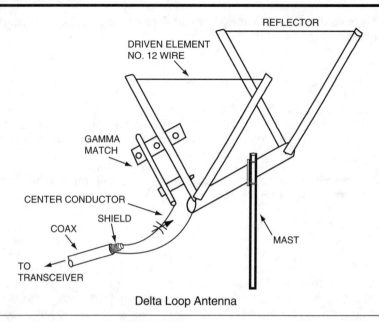

Delta Loop Antenna

G9B06 Approximately how long is each leg of a symmetrical delta-loop antenna reflector element for 14.1 MHz?
  A. 18.26 feet
  B. 23.76 feet
  C. 24.35 feet
  D. 73.05 feet
ANSWER C: Here we are looking for the reflector element of the delta-loop at 14.1 MHz. Since it's the reflector, it will be a bit longer than the driven element. Use the same formula as in the previous questions but substitute the slightly higher 1030 for 1005. Divide by the frequency in MHz. Hey, don't forget to divide by 3 because they only want one side. Calculator keystrokes are: Clear, 1030 ÷ 14.1 = 73.05 ÷ 3 = 24.35. The answer is in feet.

G9B07 Which statement about two-element delta loops and quad antennas is true?
  A. They compare favorably with a three-element Yagi
  B. They perform poorly above HF
  C. They perform very well only at HF
  D. They are effective only when constructed using insulated wire
ANSWER A: The two-element delta-loop or two-element quad compares favorably to a three-element Yagi. Try starting out with a Yagi first, and keep it relatively low to the roof line. This will help your neighbors ease into the fact that you are an amateur operator!

G9B08 Compared to a dipole antenna, what are the directional radiation characteristics of a cubical-quad antenna?
  A. The quad has more directivity in the horizontal plane but less directivity in the vertical plane
  B. The quad has less directivity in the horizontal plane but more directivity in the vertical plane

C. The quad has more directivity in both horizontal and vertical planes
D. The quad has less directivity in both horizontal and vertical planes
ANSWER C: Quads are a little bit like a magnifying glass—they have a more concentrated pattern in both the horizontal and vertical planes than any other type of antenna system.

G9B09 Moving the feed point of a multielement quad antenna from a side parallel to the ground to a side perpendicular to the ground will have what effect?
A. It will significantly increase the antenna feed-point impedance
B. It will significantly decrease the antenna feed-point impedance
C. It will change the antenna polarization from vertical to horizontal
D. It will change the antenna polarization from horizontal to vertical
ANSWER D: If we feed our quad antenna on the side perpendicular to the ground, it will change the polarization from horizontal to vertical.

G9B10 What does the term "antenna front-to-back ratio" mean in reference to a delta-loop antenna?
A. The number of directors versus the number of reflectors
B. The relative position of the driven element with respect to the reflectors and directors
C. The power radiated in the major radiation lobe compared to the power radiated in exactly the opposite direction
D. The power radiated in the major radiation lobe compared to the power radiated 90 degrees away from that direction
ANSWER C: The front-to-back ratio in a two-element delta-loop antenna is the power radiated in the main lobe compared to the power radiated in exactly the opposite direction.

G9B11 What is the "main lobe" of a delta-loop antenna radiation pattern?
A. The direction of least radiation from an antenna
B. The point of maximum current in a radiating antenna element
C. The direction of maximum radiated field strength from the antenna
D. The maximum voltage standing wave point on a radiating element
ANSWER C: The term "main lobe" on the delta-loop antenna is the direction of maximum radiated field strength.

G9C Random wire antennas—physical dimensions; impedance matching; radiation patterns; directivity and major lobes; feed point impedance of 1/2-wavelength dipole and 1/4-wavelength vertical antennas

G9C01 What type of multiband transmitting antenna does NOT require a feed-line?
A. A random-wire antenna
B. A triband Yagi antenna
C. A delta-loop antenna
D. A Beverage antenna
ANSWER A: The random wire antenna has no feed line. It begins radiating right at the output of the antenna matching device. All other antennas, like Yagis, loops, and the beverage antenna, require coax or balanced-line feed systems.

G9C02 What is one advantage of using a random-wire antenna?
A. It is more efficient than any other kind of antenna
B. It will keep RF energy out of your station
C. It doesn't need an impedance matching network
D. It is a multiband antenna
ANSWER D: With the right type of impedance matching network, the random wire antenna will work on any band.

G9C03 What is one disadvantage of a random-wire antenna?
A. It must be longer than 1 wavelength
B. You may experience RF feedback in your station
C. It usually produces vertically polarized radiation
D. You must use an inverted-T matching network for multiband operation
ANSWER B: Unless you use a remote-mounted automatic antenna tuner, the random-wire antenna can put a lot of RF feedback in your station.

G9C04 What is an advantage of downward sloping radials on a ground-plane antenna?
A. It lowers the radiation angle
B. It brings the feed-point impedance closer to 300 ohms
C. It increases the radiation angle
D. It brings the feed-point impedance closer to 50 ohms
ANSWER D: On a simple ground-plane antenna, the radials are bent down about 45 degrees to bring the feedpoint impedance close to 50 ohms. If they stick straight out, the impedance is more like 30 ohms, causing a mismatch.

G9C05 What happens to the feed-point impedance of a ground-plane antenna when its radials are changed from horizontal to downward-sloping?
A. It decreases
B. It increases
C. It stays the same
D. It approaches zero
ANSWER B: The feedpoint impedance increases from 30 ohms to 50 ohms when you bend the radials downward.

G9C06 What is the low-angle radiation pattern of an ideal half-wavelength dipole HF antenna installed a half-wavelength high, parallel to the earth?
A. It is a figure-eight at right angles to the antenna
B. It is a figure-eight off both ends of the antenna
C. It is a circle (equal radiation in all directions)
D. It is two smaller lobes on one side of the antenna, and one larger lobe on the other side
ANSWER A: The dipole gives you a figure eight pattern at right angles to the antenna wire. Reception and transmission are minimal off the ends of the wire.

G9C07 How does antenna height affect the horizontal (azimuthal) radiation pattern of a horizontal dipole HF antenna?
A. If the antenna is too high, the pattern becomes unpredictable
B. If the antenna is less than one-half wavelength high, the azimuthal pattern is almost omnidirectional

C. Antenna height has no affect on the pattern

D. If the antenna is less than one-half wavelength high, radiation off the ends of the wire is eliminated

ANSWER B: Never mount an antenna less than one-half wavelength from the earth. If you do, you will have tremendous signal distortion and an unpredictable radiation pattern with most of your signal going straight up.

G9C08 If the horizontal radiation pattern of an antenna shows a major lobe at 0 degrees and a minor lobe at 180 degrees, how would you describe the radiation pattern of this antenna?

A. Most of the signal would be radiated towards 180 degrees and a smaller amount would be radiated towards 0 degrees

B. Almost no signal would be radiated towards 0 degrees and a small amount would be radiated towards 180 degrees

C. Almost all the signal would be radiated equally towards 0 degrees and 180 degrees

D. Most of the signal would be radiated towards 0 degrees and a smaller amount would be radiated towards 180 degrees

ANSWER D: The horizontal radiation pattern of an antenna is the DIRECTION toward which the signal is radiated. If there is a major lobe at 0 degrees, and a minor lobe at 180 degrees, most of the signal is radiating toward 0 degrees, and only a small amount of signal is radiating backwards toward 180 degrees.

G9C09 If a slightly shorter parasitic element is placed 0.1 wavelength away and parallel to an HF dipole antenna mounted above ground, what effect will this have on the antenna's radiation pattern?

A. The radiation pattern will not be affected

B. A major lobe will develop in the horizontal plane, parallel to the two elements

C. A major lobe will develop in the vertical plane, away from the ground

D. A major lobe will develop in the horizontal plane, toward the parasitic element

ANSWER D: This is how the inventor of the Yagi figured out how to improve upon the dipole. By adding a director element in front of the dipole, and a reflector element behind the dipole, Professor Uda was able to concentrate the energy in just one direction. The direction of the energy will favor the shorter parasitic element.

G9C10 If a slightly longer parasitic element is placed 0.1 wavelength away and parallel to an HF dipole antenna mounted above ground, what effect will this have on the antenna's radiation pattern?

A. The radiation pattern will not be affected

B. A major lobe will develop in the horizontal plane, away from the parasitic element, toward the dipole

C. A major lobe will develop in the vertical plane, away from the ground

D. A major lobe will develop in the horizontal plane, parallel to the two elements

ANSWER B: If we put a longer parasitic element 0.1 wavelength away from the high-frequency dipole antenna, a major lobe will develop in the horizontal plane away from this longer parasitic element, which acts as a reflector.

G9C11 Where should the radial wires of a ground-mounted vertical antenna system be placed?
A. As high as possible above the ground
B. On the surface or buried a few inches below the ground
C. Parallel to the antenna element
D. At the top of the antenna

ANSWER B: Ground radial wires are important for the ground-mounted vertical antenna to establish its own counterpoise. To hear any real difference when you already have a few radials laid out per band, you must double the number of radials. If you have 2 per band, try 4. If you have 4, try 8. If you need more ground plane than 8 radials per band, try mounting your antenna on the aluminum shed in the backyard. The more ground radials you have on a ground plane antenna, the lower the angle of takeoff radiation. And this means more DX. Get out the shovel, and start digging to install more ground radials!

G9D Popular antenna feed-lines—characteristic impedance and impedance matching; SWR calculations

---

G9D01 Which of the following factors help determine the characteristic impedance of a parallel-conductor antenna feed-line?
A. The distance between the centers of the conductors and the radius of the conductors
B. The distance between the centers of the conductors and the length of the line
C. The radius of the conductors and the frequency of the signal
D. The frequency of the signal and the length of the line

ANSWER A: It's important never to squash coax cable in a window or in a car door. If you do, it will change the distance between the center conductor and the outside braid, and this changes the characteristic impedance of the cable— whether it's coax or parallel conductor feed line.

G9D02 What is the typical characteristic impedance of coaxial cables used for antenna feed-lines at amateur stations?
A. 25 and 30 ohms
B. 50 and 75 ohms
C. 80 and 100 ohms
D. 500 and 750 ohms

ANSWER B: Amateur Radio coax cable usually is rated at 50 ohms impedance. You might also use some very large TV hard-line coax cable with a proper matching network for your ham setup. Most CATV coax is rated at 75 ohms.

G9D03 What is the characteristic impedance of flat-ribbon TV-type twin-lead ?
A. 50 ohms
B. 75 ohms
C. 100 ohms
D. 300 ohms

ANSWER D: Flat-ribbon TV-type twin lead is rated at 300-ohms impedance.

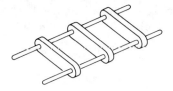

a. Parallel Two-Wire Line

b. Twisted Pair

c. Two-Wire Ribbon Flat Lead (Twin Lead)

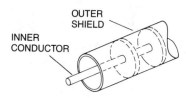

d. Air Coaxial with Washer Insulator

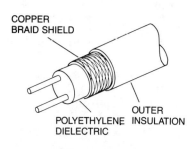

e. Two-Wire Shielded Pair

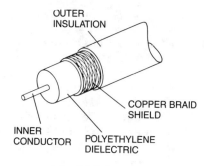

f. Coaxial (Called Coax)

Different Transmission Lines

Source: *Antennas—Selection and Installation,* © 1986 Master Publishing, Inc., Lincolnwood, IL

G9D04 What is the typical cause of power being reflected back down an antenna feed-line?

A. Operating an antenna at its resonant frequency
B. Using more transmitter power than the antenna can handle
C. A difference between feed-line impedance and antenna feed-point impedance
D. Feeding the antenna with unbalanced feed-line

ANSWER C: Keep the impedances of your feed line and antenna the same for minimum standing wave ratio. Standing waves are set up on the feed line because power is being reflected back from an impedance mismatch.

G9D05 What must be done to prevent standing waves of voltage and current on an antenna feed-line?

A. The antenna feed point must be at DC ground potential
B. The feed line must be cut to an odd number of electrical quarter-wavelengths long
C. The feed line must be cut to an even number of physical half-wavelengths long
D. The antenna feed-point impedance must be matched to the characteristic impedance of the feed-line

---

ANSWER D: Always try to match feedpoint impedance of the antenna to the characteristic impedance of the feedline for maximum power transfer and minimum SWR.

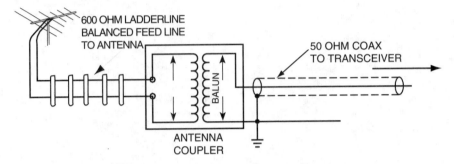

Use Antenna Coupler to Match Antenna Feedline to Coaxial Cable

Source: *Antennas—Selection and Installation,* © 1986 Master Publishing, Inc., Lincolnwood, IL

G9D06 If a center-fed dipole antenna is fed by parallel-conductor feed-line, how would an inductively coupled matching network be used in the antenna system?
    A. It would not normally be used with parallel-conductor feed-lines
    B. It would be used to increase the SWR to an acceptable level
    C. It would be used to match the unbalanced transmitter output to the balanced parallel-conductor feed-line
    D. It would be used at the antenna feed point to tune out the radiation resistance

ANSWER C: If you were to feed a center-fed dipole antenna with parallel conductor feed line, you would need a matching network to match the unbalanced transmitter output (coax) to the balanced parallel conductor feed line.

G9D07 If a 160-meter signal and a 2-meter signal pass through the same coaxial cable, how will the attenuation of the two signals compare?
    A. It will be greater at 2 meters
    B. It will be less at 2 meters
    C. It will be the same at both frequencies
    D. It will depend on the emission type in use

ANSWER A: The higher you go in frequency, the greater the attenuation of the transmission line. This is why it's very important to always use the largest size coax cable available for VHF and UHF frequencies.

G9D08 In what values are RF feed line losses usually expressed?
    A. Bels/1000 ft
    B. dB/1000 ft
    C. Bels/100 ft
    D. dB/100 ft

ANSWER D: RF feedline losses are usually expressed in decibels per 100 feet.

Frequency (MHz)	Attenuation (dB/100 ft.)
2	0.21
10	0.5
20	0.71
100	1.7
200	2.4
1000	5.7

Attenuation of RG-8 Coax with Foam Dielectric

G9D09 What standing-wave-ratio will result from the connection of a 50-ohm feed line to a resonant antenna having a 200-ohm feed-point impedance?
- A. 4:1
- B. 1:4
- C. 2:1
- D. 1:2

ANSWER A: 50 into 200 goes 4 times, so the impedance of the mismatch is 4:1. 1:4 is not the correct answer, even though it looks correct.

G9D10 What standing-wave-ratio will result from the connection of a 50-ohm feed line to a resonant antenna having a 10-ohm feed-point impedance?
- A. 2:1
- B. 50:1
- C. 1:5
- D. 5:1

ANSWER D: 10 into 50 goes 5 times, so the mismatch is 5:1. 1:5 is not correct.

G9D11 What standing-wave-ratio will result from the connection of a 50-ohm feed line to a resonant antenna having a 50-ohm feed-point impedance?
- A. 2:1
- B. 50:50
- C. 0:0
- D. 1:1

ANSWER D: 50 into 50 is a perfect match, so your SWR would be 1:1.

Subelement G0 – RF Safety
(5 exam questions – 5 topic groups)

G0A RF Safety Principles

G0A01 Depending on the wavelength of the signal, the energy density of the RF field, and other factors, in what way can RF energy affect body tissue?
- A. It heats body tissue
- B. It causes radiation poisoning

C. It causes the blood count to reach a dangerously low level

D. It cools body tissue

ANSWER A: When you reheat a slice of ham or beef in the microwave oven, what are you actually doing? The microwave oven concentrates radio signals into the meat and it heats up. If microwaves are concentrated on the human body, it heats the body tissue just like your leftovers.

G0A02 Which property is NOT important in estimating RF energy's effect on body tissue?

A. Its duty cycle

B. Its critical angle

C. Its power density

D. Its frequency

ANSWER B: The duty cycle of the incoming microwaves, their frequency, and their power density all determine how much radiofrequency energy is affecting the body tissue. The term "critical angle" has nothing to do with RF damage to the body. Critical angle deals with how radio waves enter the ionosphere.

G0A03 Which of the following has the most direct effect on the exposure level of RF radiation?

A. The maximum usable frequency of the ionosphere

B. The frequency (or wavelength) of the energy

C. The environment near the transmitter

D. The distance from the antenna

ANSWER B: The human body as a whole is resonant at frequencies from 30 MHz to 300 MHz. The frequency, or wavelength, of the radiofrequency energy has a direct effect on our exposure level to RF radiation.

G0A04 What unit of measurement best describes the biological effects of RF fields at frequencies used by amateur operators?

A. Electric field strength (V/m)

B. Magnetic field strength (A/m)

C. Specific absorption rate (W/kg)

D. Power density (W/cm^2)

ANSWER C: Remember those leftovers we warmed in the microwave? They heat up because the meat absorbs the RF energy. SAR—specific absorption rate—is a measure of the rate at which RF energy is absorbed by an incremental mass contained in a volume element of dielectric material, such as our body tissue. SAR is usually expressed in terms of watts per kilogram (W/kg) or milliwatts per gram (mW/g). Guidelines for human exposure to RF fields are based on SAR thresholds where adverse biological effects may occur. When the human body is exposed to an RF field, the SAR is proportional to the squared value of the electric field strength induced in the body.

G0A05 RF radiation in which of the following frequency ranges has the most effect on the human eyes?

A. The 3.5-MHz range

B. The 2-MHz range

C. The 50-MHz range

D. The 1270-MHz range

ANSWER D: The human eye has a relatively high resonant frequency because it is rather small and lacks blood with which to dissipate heat. RF radiation in the 1270-MHz range has the greatest effect on the human eye.

G0A06 What does the term "athermal effects" of RF radiation mean?
 A. Biological effects from RF energy other than heating
 B. Chemical effects from RF energy on minerals and liquids
 C. A change in the phase of a signal resulting from the heating of an antenna
 D. Biological effects from RF energy in excess of the maximum permissible exposure level

ANSWER A: RF radiation also can affect our body in ways other than heating tissue. This is called the ATHERMAL, or "non-thermal," effect.

G0A07 At what frequencies does the human body absorb RF energy at a maximum rate?
 A. The high-frequency (3-30-MHz) range
 B. The very-high-frequency (30-300-MHz) range
 C. The ultra-high-frequency (300-MHz to 3-GHz) range
 D. The super-high-frequency (3-GHz to 30-GHz) range

ANSWER B: While our eye is resonant near 1270 MHz, our human body resonates at a lower frequency, from 30 MHz to 300 MHz. This includes the 6-meter band at 50 MHz, the 2-meter band at 144 MHz, and is close to our UHF privileges on the 70-cm band.

G0A08 What does "time averaging" mean when it applies to RF radiation exposure?
 A. The average time of day when the exposure occurs
 B. The average time it takes RF radiation to have any long term effect on the body
 C. The total time of the exposure, e.g. 6 minutes or 30 minutes
 D. The total RF exposure averaged over a certain time

ANSWER D: Time-averaging is a method of calculating an individual's total exposure to RF radiation over a given period of time. The premise of time-averaging is that the human body can tolerate larger amounts of RF radiation if the exposure is received in short "bursts" as compared to a constant exposure at the same high level. As depicted here, total exposure to various levels of radiation is averaged over a 6-minute period. On a time-averaged basis, the amount of thermal load on the body is equal in all cases.

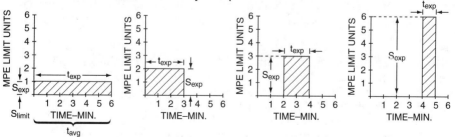

The General Equation for Time Averaging Exposure Equivalence is:

$$S_{exp}\ t_{exp} = S_{limit}\ t_{avg}$$

G0A09 What guideline is used to determine whether or not a routine RF evaluation must be performed for an amateur station?
   A. If the transmitter's PEP is 50 watts or more, an evaluation must always be performed
   B. If the RF radiation from the antenna system falls within a controlled environment, an evaluation must be performed
   C. If the RF radiation from the antenna system falls within an uncontrolled environment, an evaluation must be performed
   D. If the transmitter's PEP and frequency are within certain limits given in Part 97, an evaluation must be performed

ANSWER D: Federal Communications Commission rules state that: "The licensee must perform the routine RF environmental evaluation prescribed by Section 1.1307(b) of this chapter, if the power of the licensee's station exceeds the following PEP limits:"

Wavelength Band	Power Input Limit	Wavelength Band	Power Input Limit
160 meters	500	10 meters	50
80 meters	500	6 meters	50
75 meters	500	2 meters	50
40 meters	500	1.25 meters	50
30 meters	425	70 cm	70
20 meters	225	33 cm	150
17 meters	125	23 cm	200
15 meters	100	13 cm	250
12 meters	75	All SHF & EHF	250

FCC Limits on Power Input to Antenna in Watts by Band

G0A10 If you perform a routine RF evaluation on your station and determine that its RF fields exceed the FCC's exposure limits in human-accessible areas, what are you required to do?
   A. Take action to prevent human exposure to the excessive RF fields
   B. File an Environmental Impact Statement (EIS-97) with the FCC
   C. Secure written permission from your neighbors to operate above the controlled MPE limits
   D. Nothing; simply keep the evaluation in your station records

ANSWER A: When you perform your routine RF evaluation on your ham station and determine that the RF fields exceed FCC exposure limits, you must take measures to prevent human exposure to the excessive RF fields. Such measures could include raising your antenna higher or installing a wooden fence with warning signs.

G0A11 At a site with multiple transmitters operating at the same time, how is each transmitter included in the RF exposure site evaluation?
   A. Only the RF field of the most powerful transmitter need be considered
   B. The RF fields of all transmitters are multiplied together
   C. Transmitters that produce more than 5% of the maximum permissible power density exposure limit for that transmitter must be included
   D. Only the RF fields from any transmitters operating with high duty-cycle modes (greater than 50%) need to be considered

ANSWER C: Station owners operating repeaters need to do careful calculations to ensure that the addition of their transmitter won't cause the entire repeater site to reach overexposure. Each transmitter is included in the RF exposure site evaluation if it produces more than 5% of the maximum permissible power limit for that transmitter. Remember "5%" and notice that all the other answers are different.

G0B RF Safety Rules and Guidelines

G0B01 What are the FCC's RF-safety rules designed to control?
- A. The maximum RF radiated electric field strength
- B. The maximum RF radiated magnetic field strength
- C. The maximum permissible human exposure to all RF radiated fields
- D. The maximum RF radiated power density

ANSWER C: The Federal Communications Commission RF-safety rules have been specifically formulated to protect us and those around us from overexposure to any type of RF radiated fields from a nearby antenna.

G0B02 At a site with multiple transmitters, who must ensure that all FCC RF-safety regulations are met?
- A. All licensees contributing more than 5% of the maximum permissible power density exposure for that transmitter are equally responsible
- B. Only the licensee of the station producing the strongest RF field is responsible
- C. All of the stations at the site are equally responsible, regardless of any station's contribution to the total RF field
- D. Only the licensees of stations which are producing an RF field exceeding the maximum permissible exposure limit are responsible

ANSWER A: If the transmitter produces more than 5% of the maximum permissible power, the station owner must ensure that all FCC RF-safety regulations for the entire site are met. Owners of repeater stations with antennas on towers atop buildings must conduct a "roofline" RF safety evaluation if the effective radiated power (ERP) exceeds 500 watts. See answer at G0A09.

G0B03 What effect does duty cycle have when evaluating RF exposure?
- A. Low duty-cycle emissions permit greater short-term exposure levels
- B. High duty-cycle emissions permit greater short-term exposure levels
- C. The duty cycle is not considered when evaluating RF exposure
- D. Any duty cycle may be used as long as it is less than 100 percent

ANSWER A: Duty cycle is the percentage of time the transmitter is actually sending out energy. If you hold down your telegraph key for continuous full transmit power output, this would be 100% duty cycle. If the space in between each dit were equal to the duration of the transmitted signal, this would be a 50% duty cycle. The lower duty cycle will permit greater short-term exposure levels to RF radiation.

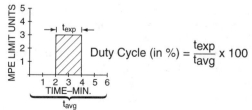

$$\text{Duty Cycle (in \%)} = \frac{t_{exp}}{t_{avg}} \times 100$$

G0B04 What is the threshold power used to determine if an RF environmental evaluation is required when the operation takes place in the 15-meter band?

    A. 50 watts PEP
    B. 100 watts PEP
    C. 225 watts PEP
    D. 500 watts PEP

ANSWER B: Look again at the Table at G0A09 showing the wavelength bands and peak envelope power limits. On the 15-meter band, the threshold power between no evaluation or evaluation is 100 watts. 100 watts is about all you're going to get out of a regular worldwide mobile transceiver.

G0B05 Why do the power levels used to determine if an RF environmental evaluation is required vary with frequency?

    A. Because amateur operators may use a variety of power levels
    B. Because Maximum Permissible Exposure (MPE) limits are frequency dependent
    C. Because provision must be made for signal loss due to propagation
    D. All of these choices are correct

ANSWER B: Maximum permissible exposure limits are frequency dependent because different parts of our body are resonant to strong RF fields on different bands. Some parts of the body are more susceptible to RF energy—such as the eyes and testes—since they lack an adequate blood supply with which to dissipate heat. This is why there are lower power levels on the 10-, 6-, and 2-meter bands than on longer wavelength frequencies.

G0B06 What is the threshold power used to determine if an RF environmental evaluation is required when the operation takes place in the 10-meter band?

    A. 50 watts PEP
    B. 100 watts PEP
    C. 225 watts PEP
    D. 500 watts PEP

ANSWER A: The human body absorbs RF energy best between 30 and 300 MHz. The 10-meter band is very close to 30-MHz, so it has the lowest threshold power level.

G0B07 What is the threshold power used to determine if an RF environmental evaluation is required for transmissions in the amateur bands with frequencies less than 10 MHz?

    A. 50 watts PEP
    B. 100 watts PEP
    C. 225 watts PEP
    D. 500 watts PEP

ANSWER D: We can run up to 500 watts on the 160-, 80-, 75- and 40-meter bands before the routine RF Safety evaluation is required.

G0B08 What amateur frequency bands have the lowest power limits above which an RF environmental evaluation is required?

    A. All bands between 17 and 30 meters
    B. All bands between 10 and 15 meters

C. All bands between 40 and 160 meters

D. All bands between 1.25 and 10 meters

ANSWER D: The lowest power level limits occur on the 10-meter and our popular VHF/UHF repeater bands; 6m, 2m, and the 222-MHz band.

G0B09 What is the threshold power used to determine if an RF safety evaluation is required when the operation takes place in the 20-meter band?

A. 50 watts PEP

B. 100 watts PEP

C. 225 watts PEP

D. 500 watts PEP

ANSWER C: On the 20-meter band, you need to throttle back to 225 watts peak envelope power output at the antenna in order to stay below the RF safety evaluation requirements threshold.

G0B10 Under what conditions would an RF environmental evaluation be required for an amateur repeater station where the transmitting antenna is NOT mounted on a building?

A. The repeater transmitter is activated for more than 6 minutes without 30 seconds pauses

B. The height above ground to the lowest point of the antenna is less than 10 m and the radiated power from the antenna exceeds 500 W ERP

C. The height above ground to the lowest point of the antenna is less than 2 m and the radiated power from the antenna exceeds 500 W ERP

D. When the radiated power from the antenna exceeds 50 W ERP

ANSWER B: This is a good question for those of you who might want to become a repeater station trustee. If your repeater antenna is mounted less than about 30 feet (10 meters) above the ground, or if you are running a real powerful base station collinear antenna that exceeds 500 watts effective radiated power, then you WILL need to conduct an RF environmental evaluation. Because the antenna is NOT mounted on a building, people can get closer to it—entering the "near field"—and exposing themselves to RF radiation. Get that antenna higher up, or put a fence around it with warning signs to keep people out of the "near field."

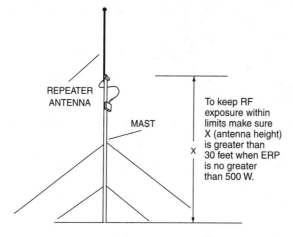

To keep RF exposure within limits make sure X (antenna height) is greater than 30 feet when ERP is no greater than 500 W.

Repeater Antenna Installation

G0B11 Under what conditions would an RF environmental evaluation be required for an amateur repeater station where the transmitting antenna is mounted on a building?
- A. The repeater transmitter is activated for more than 6 minutes without 30 seconds pauses
- B. The height above ground to the lowest point of the antenna is less than 10 m and the radiated power from the antenna exceeds 50 W ERP
- C. The height above ground to the lowest point of the antenna is less than 2 m and the radiated power from the antenna exceeds 50 W ERP
- D. The radiated power from the antenna exceeds 500 W ERP

ANSWER D: Now that antenna is on top of a building, which acts as a shield and keeps people away from it. The very big and expensive base-station repeater antennas usually offer as much as 10-dB gain. This will lead to an effective radiated power of 10 times the repeater output power. Most repeaters nominally run 50 watts of power. This puts you right at the edge at 500 watts ERP for the RF environmental evaluation when your antenna is mounted on a building. Slightly reduce power output into that 10-dB gain antenna, and stay below the 500-watt ERP threshold.

G0C Routine Station Evaluation and Measurements (FCC Part 97 refers to RF Radiation Evaluation)

G0C01 If the free-space far-field strength of a 10-MHz dipole antenna measures 1.0 millivolts per meter at a distance of 5 wavelengths, what will the field strength measure at a distance of 10 wavelengths?
- A. 0.10 millivolts per meter
- B. 0.25 millivolts per meter
- C. 0.50 millivolts per meter
- D. 1.0 millivolts per meter

ANSWER C: Don't panic! You can calculate field strength measurements in your head on these 5 questions. Just remember that in the far-field region, the field strength is inversely proportional to an increase in distance. Don't concern yourself with the frequency or type of antenna for these problems.

If a calibrated field-strength meter is used for far-field strength measurements, we will go by the common assumption that ground waves over sea water or a flat terrain decrease in field strength INVERSELY as the distance from the antenna increases. This is particularly true in low- and medium-frequency ranges. In this first question, the distance gets doubled, so field strength gets halved. One millivolt will now read only 0.5 millivolts at twice the distance.

G0C02 If the free-space far-field strength of a 28-MHz Yagi antenna measures 4.0 millivolts per meter at a distance of 5 wavelengths, what will the field strength measure at a distance of 20 wavelengths?
- A. 2.0 millivolts per meter
- B. 1.0 millivolts per meter
- C. 0.50 millivolts per meter
- D. 0.25 millivolts per meter

ANSWER B: In this question, we increase our distance by 4 times, causing only 1/4 of the original 4 millivolts to finally reach our new location. 4 millivolts will now read 1 millivolt per meter with a 4 times increase in distance.

G0C03 If the free-space far-field strength of a 1.8-MHz dipole antenna measures 9 microvolts per meter at a distance of 4 wavelengths, what will the field strength measure at a distance of 12 wavelengths?
    A. 3 microvolts per meter
    B. 3.6 microvolts per meter
    C. 4.8 microvolts per meter
    D. 10 microvolts per meter
ANSWER A: In this problem, our distance increases by 3 times, so we will only have 1/3 of 9 millivolts per meter field strength at the new location—giving us only 3 microvolts per meter.

G0C04 If the free-space far-field power density of a 18-MHz Yagi antenna measures 10 milliwatts per square meter at a distance of 3 wavelengths, what will it measure at a distance of 6 wavelengths?
    A. 11 milliwatts per square meter
    B. 5.0 milliwatts per square meter
    C. 3.3 milliwatts per square meter
    D. 2.5 milliwatts per square meter
ANSWER D: Be sure to read this question carefully! Instead of asking for field strength, they want to know *power density*. To refresh your memory, here is the formula for Power Density, S, for the far-field region:

$$S = \frac{PG}{4\pi R^2}$$

Where S is power density in W/m²
    P is power input in Watts
    G is gain of antenna relative to isotropic radiator (a ratio)
    R is distance to the center of radiation in meters (m)

The power density in the far-field, or Fraunhofer region, of an antenna pattern decreases INVERSELY as the SQUARE of the distance. In this case, the distance was doubled which will result in a 4 times decrease of far-field power density. 1/4 of 10 milliwatts is 2.5 milliwatts per square meter.

G0C05 If the free-space far-field power density of an antenna measures 9 milliwatts per square meter at a distance of 5 wavelengths, what will the field strength measure at a distance of 15 wavelengths?
    A. 3 milliwatts per square meter
    B. 1 milliwatt per square meter
    C. 0.9 milliwatt per square meter
    D. 0.09 milliwatt per square meter
ANSWER B: In this problem, they again are asking for power density, not far-field strength. Keep in mind that power density in the far-field decreases *inversely* as the *square* of the distance. In this case, we have increased the distance 3 times (5 wavelengths to 15 wavelengths), and the square of 3 is 9. 9 divided by 9 gives us 1 milliwatt per square meter. Got it? You can do these in your head—but watch out, if you accidentally mix up field strength with power density, they have a wrong answer just waiting for you to think it is the correct one.

G0C06 What factors determine the location of the boundary between the near and far fields of an antenna?
A. Wavelength of the signal and physical size of the antenna
B. Antenna height and element material
C. Boom length and element material
D. Transmitter power and antenna gain

ANSWER A: The largest factors that determine the boundary between near- and far-field are the wavelength of the signal and the physical size of the antenna.

G0C07 Which of the following steps might an amateur operator take to ensure compliance with the RF safety regulations?
A. Post a copy of FCC Part 97 in the station
B. Post a copy of OET Bulletin 65 in the station
C. Nothing; amateur compliance is voluntary
D. Perform a routine RF exposure evaluation

ANSWER D: Performing a routine RF exposure evaluation is a good idea for all amateurs to ensure compliance with RF-safety regulations, and to ensure that you and your neighbors are not becoming "overexposed" to RF radiation.

G0C08 In the free-space far field, what is the relationship between the electric field (E field) and magnetic field (H field)?
A. The electric field strength is equal to the square of the magnetic field strength
B. The electric field strength is equal to the cube of the magnetic field strength
C. The electric and magnetic field strength has a fixed impedance relationship of 377 ohms
D. The electric field strength times the magnetic field strength equals 377 ohms

ANSWER C: It can be mathematically proven that the impedance relationship between the electric and magnetic fields is 377 ohms. Since the formula for Power Density is:

$$S = \frac{E^2}{3770} = 37.7 \, H^2$$

$$E^2 = 3770 \times 37.7 \, H^2$$

$$\frac{E^2}{H^2} = 142129$$

$$\frac{E}{H} = \sqrt{142129} = 377 \text{ ohms}$$

Where S = Power density in mW/cm²
E = Electric field strength in Volts/meter
H = Magnetic field strength in amperes/meter

$$\frac{E}{H} = \frac{\text{Volts/m}}{\text{amps/m}} = \frac{\text{Volts}}{\text{amps}} = \text{ohms}$$

The FIXED impedance relationship between the electric field strength and the magnetic field strength is 377 ohms. This is a FIXED IMPEDANCE, and it's a ratio, so watch out that you don't accidentally spot the "377" and go for Answer D, which is not the correct answer. Keep in mind that this is a FIXED IMPEDANCE ratio.

G0C09 What type of instrument can be used to accurately measure an RF field?
 A. A receiver with an S meter
 B. A calibrated field-strength meter with a calibrated antenna
 C. A betascope with a dummy antenna calibrated at 50 ohms
 D. An oscilloscope with a high-stability crystal marker generator

ANSWER B: Although a simple field-strength meter can show the presence of radiofrequency emissions, it takes a precisely CALIBRATED field-strength meter with a CALIBRATED antenna to accurately measure RF fields.

G0C10 If your station complies with the RF safety rules and you reduce its power output from 500 to 40 watts, how would the RF safety rules apply to your operations?
 A. You would need to reevaluate your station for compliance with the RF safety rules because the power output changed
 B. You would need to reevaluate your station for compliance with the RF safety rules because the transmitting parameters changed
 C. You would not need to perform an RF safety evaluation, but your station would still need to be in compliance with the RF safety rules
 D. The RF safety rules would no longer apply to your station because it would be operating with less than 50 watts of power

ANSWER C: One way to minimize your personal exposure to strong RF fields is to reduce power output. If you comply with the RF safety rules at 500 watts, you would also comply at a lesser power level.

G0C11 If your station complies with the RF safety rules and you reduce its power output from 1000 to 500 watts, how would the RF safety rules apply to your operations?
 A. You would need to reevaluate your station for compliance with the RF safety rules because the power output changed
 B. You would need to reevaluate your station for compliance with the RF safety rules because the transmitting parameters changed
 C. You would need to perform an RF safety evaluation to ensure your station would still be in compliance with the RF safety rules
 D. Since your station was in compliance with RF safety rules at a higher power output, you need to do nothing more

ANSWER D: Luckily, your antenna is well away from any living thing, and your station originally complied with the RF safety rules at 1,000 watts. If you reduce down to 500 watts, you don't need to do an RF safety check because you were originally in compliance at the higher level.

G0D Practical RF-safety applications

G0D01 Considering RF safety, what precaution should you take if you install an indoor transmitting antenna?
 A. Locate the antenna close to your operating position to minimize feed line losses
 B. Position the antenna along the edge of a wall where it meets the floor or ceiling to reduce parasitic radiation

C. Locate the antenna as far away as possible from living spaces that will be occupied while you are operating

D. Position the antenna parallel to electrical power wires to take advantage of parasitic effects

ANSWER C: It's always a good idea to locate an antenna as far away as possible from living spaces that will be occupied when you are transmitting on the air. If you're just receiving, no problem—but when you're transmitting, to minimize RF exposure get your wire antenna away from everyone!

G0D02 Considering RF safety, what precaution should you take whenever you make adjustments to the feed line of a directional antenna system?

A. Be sure no one can activate the transmitter

B. Disconnect the antenna-positioning mechanism

C. Point the antenna away from the sun so it doesn't concentrate solar energy on you

D. Be sure you and the antenna structure are properly grounded

ANSWER A: If you're working on the feedline or actually working on the feedpoint of a directional antenna, *be sure that no one can activate the transmitter!*

G0D03 What is the best reason to place a protective fence around the base of a ground-mounted transmitting antenna?

A. To reduce the possibility of persons being exposed to levels of RF in excess of the maximum permissible exposure (MPE) limits

B. To reduce the possibility of animals damaging the antenna

C. To reduce the possibility of persons vandalizing expensive equipment

D. To improve the antenna's grounding system and thereby reduce the possibility of lightning damage

ANSWER A: You may wish to put up a protective wooden fence around the base of a ground-mounted antenna. This will reduce the possibility of persons or your favorite pets getting too close to the antenna when you are transmitting.

G0D04 What RF-safety precautions should you take before beginning repairs on an antenna?

A. Be sure you and the antenna structure are grounded

B. Be sure to turn off the transmitter and disconnect the feed-line

C. Inform your neighbors so they are aware of your intentions

D. Turn off the main power switch in your house

ANSWER B: If you're going to be working on an antenna system, disconnect the feedline from the transmitter so there is absolutely no way that someone could accidentally transmit while you are aloft repairing the antenna.

G0D05 What precaution should be taken when installing a ground-mounted antenna?

A. It should not be installed higher than you can reach

B. It should not be installed in a wet area

C. It should be painted so people or animals do not accidentally run into it

D. It should be installed so no one can be exposed to RF radiation in excess of the maximum permissible exposure (MPE) limits

ANSWER D: There are all sorts of great 5-band and 7-band trap vertical antennas that work nicely on the ground, or on a metal shed just above the ground.

When you're looking for a spot to mount the antenna, keep in mind maximum permissible exposure limits and install it so that no one can actually walk up to it, or stand near it when you are transmitting. This goes for your pets, too. Don't fry Fido or Feline by leaving a ground-mounted vertical unfenced.

G0D06 What precaution should you take before beginning repairs on a microwave feed horn or waveguide?

- A. Wear tight-fitting clothes and gloves to protect your body and hands from sharp edges
- B. Be sure the transmitter is turned off and the power source is disconnected
- C. Wait until the weather is dry and sunny
- D. Be sure propagation conditions are not favorable for troposphere ducting

ANSWER B: Your author does a lot of work at 10 GHz, a fascinating band where small amounts of microwave energy go quite a distance. Anytime someone works on a dish or horn antenna, make sure that the transmitter is not only turned off, but also disconnected from the power source, to make absolutely sure that no one can energize the equipment while another person is working on it.

G0D07 Why should directional high-gain antennas be mounted higher than nearby structures?

- A. To eliminate inversion of the major and minor lobes
- B. So they will not damage nearby structures with RF energy
- C. So they will receive more sky waves and fewer ground waves
- D. So they will not direct excessive amounts of RF energy toward people in nearby structures

ANSWER D: When you are planning that new tri-band, 5-element, beam antenna to get onto the worldwide bands with your new General Class privileges in a BIG WAY, do a visual check to make absolutely sure you're not going to be beaming any of this energy into your own shack or your next door neighbor's upstairs bedroom. Get your antenna up as high as possible, and get it a lot higher than nearby structures. And watch for wires! Make sure you never erect an antenna where it might fall on power lines. You could be killed if your antenna comes in contact with power lines!

G0D08 For best RF safety, where should the ends and center of a dipole antenna be located?

- A. Near or over moist ground so RF energy will be radiated away from the ground
- B. As close to the transmitter as possible so RF energy will be concentrated near the transmitter
- C. As far away as possible to minimize RF exposure to people near the antenna
- D. Close to the ground so simple adjustments can be easily made without climbing a ladder

ANSWER C: A dipole antenna is a great way to get on the air without spending more than a few bucks. Just make sure that the ends and center of the dipole are as far away as possible from anyone standing around to minimize RF exposure.

G0D09 What should you do to reduce RF radiation exposure when operating at 1270 MHz?
   A. Make sure that an RF leakage filter is installed at the antenna feed point
   B. Keep the antenna away from your eyes when RF is applied
   C. Make sure the standing wave ratio is low before you conduct a test
   D. Never use a shielded horizontally polarized antenna

ANSWER B: Now we're back to 1270 MHz where your author regularly runs a Southern California repeater at 1282.400 MHz. Since 1270 MHz is close to eye-ball resonance, make absolutely sure to keep the antenna directed away from any eyes when transmitting on your handheld transceiver. As for your author's 1282.400 MHz repeater antenna, it's up quite high to minimize RF exposure.

G0D10 For best RF safety for driver and passengers, where should the antenna of a mobile VHF transceiver be mounted?
   A. On the right side of a metal rear bumper
   B. On the left side of a metal rear bumper
   C. In the center of a metal roof
   D. On the top-center of the rear window glass

ANSWER C: On VHF, the very best ground plane can be established by putting the antenna in the center of a metal roof. But in the real world of radio and new cars, most of you will go with some sort of a permanent mount where you're not drilling a hole in the center of your roof. Put the antenna somewhere up at roof level using one of those new gutter or lip mounts because the metal roof acts as a shield against RF exposure. Get that antenna as far away from everyone in the car as possible.

G0D11 Considering RF safety, which of the following is the best reason to mount the antenna of a mobile VHF transceiver in the center of a metal roof?
   A. The roof will greatly shield the driver and passengers from RF radiation
   B. The antenna will be out of the driver's line of sight
   C. The center of a metal roof is the sturdiest mounting place for an antenna
   D. The wind resistance of the antenna will be centered between the wheels and not drag on one side or the other

ANSWER A: Put the VHF antenna in the center of your metal roof. It is the safest spot for shielding everyone inside your car. But don't open your sun roof while you are transmitting!

G0E RF-safety solutions

G0E01 If you receive minor burns every time you touch your microphone while you are transmitting, which of the following statements is true?
   A. You need to use a low-impedance microphone
   B. You and others in your station may be exposed to more than the maximum permissible level of RF radiation
   C. You need to use a surge suppressor on your station transmitter
   D. All of these choices are correct

ANSWER B: Modern high-frequency and VHF microphones usually incorporate a plastic face and a metal mike clip on the top or on the back. If this metal clip is connected with a ground wire, a poorly installed transceiver will sometimes "bite you" on transmit. This is caused by RF getting into the microphone circuit and manifesting itself as a slight tingling or an actual burn to the palm of your hand when talking into the microphone. This should alert you that there is too much RF floating around your vehicle or shack, and you need to figure out what's wrong and fix it to decrease your exposure to RF radiation.

G0E02 If measurements indicate that individuals in your station are exposed to more than the maximum permissible level of radiation, which of the following corrective measures would be effective?
    A. Ensure proper grounding of the equipment
    B. Ensure that all equipment covers are tightly fastened
    C. Use the minimum amount of transmitting power necessary
    D. All of these choices are correct
ANSWER D: Good grounding techniques will help minimize "mike burns." Make sure that your equipment covers are all screwed down nice and tight, and avoid using maximum power for most of your communications.

G0E03 If calculations show that you and your family may be receiving more than the maximum permissible RF radiation exposure from your 20-meter indoor dipole, which of the following steps might be appropriate?
    A. Use RTTY instead of CW or SSB voice emissions
    B. Move the antenna to a safe outdoor environment
    C. Use an antenna-matching network to reduce your transmitted SWR
    D. All of these choices are correct
ANSWER B: Can you stand on your tippy toes and reach that indoor antenna? If so, you are too close during transmit. You should move the antenna to a safe outdoor environment to minimize exposure to yourself, your family, and your pets.

G0E04 Considering RF exposure, which of the following steps should you take when installing an antenna?
    A. Install the antenna as high and far away from populated areas as possible
    B. If the antenna is a gain antenna, point it away from populated areas
    C. Minimize feed line radiation into populated areas
    D. All of these choices are correct
ANSWER D: Always try to mount your antenna as high as possible, and as far away from where anyone will be standing, seated, or sleeping. If you're running a Yagi antenna, make sure it's not pointed directly at your neighbors. And when you run your feedlines—especially ladder line—make absolutely sure it's well away from areas where anybody is standing, seated, or sleeping!

G0E05 What might you do if an RF radiation evaluation shows that your neighbors may be receiving more than the maximum RF radiation exposure limit from your Yagi antenna when it is pointed at their house?
    A. Change from horizontal polarization to vertical polarization
    B. Change from horizontal polarization to circular polarization

   C. Use an antenna with a higher front to rear ratio
   D. Take precautions to ensure you can't point your antenna at their house

ANSWER D: If your calculations indicate you may be exposing your neighbors to too much RF, you may need to relocate your entire antenna system, or take precautions to ensure it cannot be pointed at their house when transmitting.

G0E06 What might you do if an RF radiation evaluation shows that your neighbors may be receiving more than the maximum RF radiation exposure limit from your quad antenna when it is pointed at their house?
   A. Reduce your transmitter power to a level that reduces their exposure to a value below the maximum permissible exposure (MPE) limit
   B. Change from horizontal polarization to vertical polarization
   C. Use an antenna with a higher front to side ratio
   D. Use an antenna with a sharper radiation lobe

ANSWER A: If you find that you are exceeding the RF radiation exposure limits, immediately reduce transmitter power to well below the maximum permissible exposure limit.

G0E07 Why does a dummy antenna provide an RF safe environment for transmitter adjusting?
   A. The dummy antenna carries the RF energy far away from the station before releasing it
   B. The RF energy is contained in a halo around the outside of the dummy antenna
   C. The RF energy is not radiated from a dummy antenna, but is converted to heat
   D. The dummy antenna provides a perfect match to the antenna feed impedance

ANSWER C: The good dummy load antenna is encased in a metal cage or can. It dissipates the RF energy as heat, keeps the RF energy from escaping, thus protecting you and your neighbors from overexposure.

G0E08 From an RF radiation exposure point of view, which of the following materials would be the best to use for your homemade transmatch enclosure?
   A. Aluminum
   B. Bakelite
   C. Transparent acrylic plastic
   D. Any nonconductive material

ANSWER A: If you're going to build your own antenna coupler, make sure it's constructed with a metal (aluminum) enclosure to minimize RF radiation leakage. This is why the cabinet of your microwave oven is made of metal.

G0E09 From an RF radiation exposure point of view, what is the advantage to using a high-gain, narrow-beamwidth antenna for your VHF station?
   A. High-gain antennas absorb stray radiation
   B. The RF radiation can be better focused in a direction away from populated areas

C. Narrow-beamwidth antennas eliminate exposure in areas directly under the antenna

D. All of these choices are correct

ANSWER B: One advantage to a long-boom, high-gain, VHF antenna is that you can better focus the radiated energy in a direction away from your neighbors.

G0E10 From an RF radiation exposure point of view, what is the disadvantage in using a high-gain, narrow-beamwidth antenna for your VHF station?

A. High-gain antennas must be fed with coaxial cable feed-line, which radiates stray RF energy

B. The RF radiation can be better focused in a direction away from populated areas

C. Individuals in the main beam of the radiation pattern will receive a greater exposure than when a low-gain antenna is used

D. All of these choices are correct

ANSWER C: One disadvantage to using a high-gain, narrow-beamwidth antenna is that you could inadvertently point it at your neighbor's house and overexpose them to RF radiation.

G0E11 If your station is located in a residential area, which of the following would best help you reduce the RF exposure to your neighbors from your amateur station?

A. Use RTTY instead of CW or SSB voice emissions

B. Install your antenna as high as possible to maximize the distance to nearby people

C. Use top-quality coaxial cable to reduce RF losses in the feed-line

D. Use an antenna matching network to reduce your transmitted SWR

ANSWER B: This is your final question in preparation for General Class! When the neighbors spot you putting that big antenna up on your roof, tell them you need to get it up as high as possible in order to provide everyone with a good, safe RF environment. The higher the better. Tell them that all that aluminum in the air is really a work of art. After all, that big, new huge beam is announcing that you have successfully prepared for your General Class license, and that you will be on the airwaves soon with a powerful, but absolutely safe, signal.

REVIEW TIME

Now that you have completed your first pass through all of the new General Class questions, begin to check off those questions that you know perfectly. But double check your work—there are many distracters that look very close to the correct answers!

We strongly recommend that you obtain a copy of the Amateur Radio Relay League's *ARRL Handbook for Radio Amateurs.* It contains a great deal of information on proper Amateur Radio operating practices, electrical principles, and engineering.

Welcome (in advance) to the high-frequency worldwide bands. If you study the material in this book, and practice your Morse code skills, you'll do just fine on your written examination and CW code test!

AN IMPORTANT WORD ABOUT RF SAFETY

In 1996, the Federal Communications Commission adopted new guidelines and procedures for evaluating human exposure to environmental radio-frequency (RF) electromagnetic fields from FCC-regulated transmitters, including those operated by amateurs. As a result, a new subelement 0 on RF Safety has been added to the Novice (Element 2), Technician (Element 3A), and General Class (Element 3B) licensing examinations. Many of the subelement 0 questions in the new General Class, Element 3B, examination assume knowledge based on the questions from the Novice and Technician Class examinations that became effective July 1, 1997.

If you passed your Novice and Technician Class written examinations prior to July 1, 1997, you may wish to obtain a copy of *Technician No-Code Plus*, by Gordon West (Radio Shack #62-2426). It includes the Element 1A and 1B questions, answers, and explanations regarding RF safety, as well as the FCC data tables for determining near-field and far-field RF emission strength and other important RF safety information. Reviewing that material will be helpful to you in studying for and passing your General Class examination.

The new RF safety rules also require that amateur radio facilities are subject to routine RF environmental evaluation when they are operated above certain power levels (the reason for question G0A09). A lengthier discussion of RF exposure standards, and tables to help you evaluate the RF safety of your amateur station installation, are included in the Appendix (see pages 131 to 133).

To read the full story about RF safety for the radio amateur, visit the FCC website at: http://www.fcc.gov/oet/rfsafety. This is where you will find OST/OET Bulletin No. 65, *Evaluating Compliance with FCC Guidelines for Human Exposure to Radio Frequency Electromagnetic Fields*, plus any supplements for the amateur radio operator. While you may not want to download this lengthy, in-depth document, you should review it so you understand the importance of staying away from an amateur antenna when the operator is actually transmitting.

The FCC relies on the skills and demonstrated abilities of amateur operators to comply with all of its technical rules, including those on RF safety. Complying with these rules will help assure that you and your neighbors are protected from all the ill effects of RF radiation. Please, stay safe around any antenna system that is on-the-air transmitting radiofrequency (RF) energy.

4

Taking the General Class Examination

ABOUT THIS CHAPTER

Get ready for worldwide privileges! As soon as you pass your General Class theory exam and code test (and if you hold a valid Technician or Technician-Plus license) you can broadcast on frequency bands that let you talk to the world every hour of the day and night. This chapter tells you how the examination will be given, who is qualified to administer it, and what happens after you successfully complete the written exam and code test.

THE GENERAL CLASS EXAMINATION

Here is an overview of the General Class examination and what to expect when you go to the test session.

Examination Administration

The General Class examination is given by a team of three Volunteer Examiners (VEs). They are hams who hold Advanced or Extra Class licenses and are accredited to administer your examination and code test by a Volunteer Examiner Coordinator (VEC).

Volunteer Examiner Teams offer examinations on a regular basis at local sites to serve their communities. Generally, the VETs closely coordinate their activities with one another and rotate examination sites, so you should be able to find a nearby test site and exam date that is convenient for you. You can obtain information about VETs and exam sessions in your area by checking with your local radio club, ham radio store, or local packet bulletin boards. Your local Radio Shack store manager also may be able to help you find a nearby test location and date. If this is not convenient, call or write the VEC that serves your area. A list of VECs that was current at the time of publication is given in the Appendix (see page 120).

Once you have found your local VET, contact them to select a test date and location and pre-register for your examination. They will hold a seat for you at the next available session, and they will appreciate you contacting them ahead of time to make a reservation. Don't be a no-show, and don't be a surprise-show. Call them ahead of time and pre-register!

The Volunteer Examiners are not compensated for their time and skills, but they are permitted to charge you a fee for certain reimbursable expenses incurred in preparing, administering, and processing the examination. The maximum fee is adjusted annually by the FCC and currently is about $6.25.

Exam Content

The questions, answers, and distracters for each question of the General Class written examination are public information. The question pool included in the book contains all 332 possible questions that can be used to make up your 30-question Element 3B written examination. The VET *is not permitted* to change any of the wording, punctuation or numerical values included in any questions, answers, or distracters. The VET *is allowed* to change the A, B, C, D order of the answers, if it wishes.

Also, the VET is not required to select one question from each syllabus topic under each subelement. For example, it could use two questions from G9A — Yagi antennas, and no question from G9B — Loop antennas. However, this is discouraged because many of the questions within the same syllabus topic are duplicate questions asked in different ways. You should expect a written exam that contains one question from each syllabus topic within each subelement. Look again at the question pool syllabus on page 19 to see how the test will be constructed.

Taking the Examination

First, get a good night's sleep before examination day! Continue to study right up to the moment you go into the examination room. Make sure to review those questions that you have had difficulty remembering. If you plan to take the code test on the same day you take your written examination, listen to the code tapes while you drive to the test site. Don't believe that old saying that too much study will cause you to forget subject material.

What to Bring to the Site

Here's what you'll need to bring with you for your General Class examination:

- The examination fee of approximately $6.25 in cash, exact change. No checks accepted.
- The original plus two copies of your current Technician or Technician-Plus license. If your license has not yet arrived, make sure you bring the original plus two copies of your Certificate of Successful Completion of Examination (CSCE) indicating your most current license status.
- A photo identification card — your driver's license is ideal for this purpose.
- Some sharp pencils and fine-tip pens. It's good to have a backup.
- Calculators may be used. However, the examiners may erase the memory before your exam begins.
- Any other items that the VET asks you to bring.

NOTE: If you are requesting a handicapped exemption from the 13-wpm Morse code test, or need a special exam because of your handicap, obtain a letter from your physician attesting to the nature of your handicap and bring it with you to the exam session. If you need special equipment, you must supply it. Also, if you do have a handicap, let your VET know this when you call to pre-register for your exam. That way, you'll know what they would like you to bring and they will be better able to accommodate your needs. (See page 4 for information on Morse code exemptions granted to handicapped ham operators by the FCC.)

During the Exam

Don't speed read the examination! Read each question carefully. Take your time looking for the correct answer. Some answers start out looking correct, but end up wrong. When you finish, go back over every question and double-check your answers.

When you are satisfied that you have passed the examination, turn in all of your test papers to the examination team. Make sure to thank them and to let them know how much you appreciate their unselfish efforts to help promote our hobby. And, if you're the last person out of the room, volunteer to help take down the testing location. They'll appreciate your offer.

After the Exam

Wait patiently outside the exam room for your results. Chances are the VEs will greet you with a smile and your CSCE. (If you didn't pass, they will tell you what to do next.) When you are told you passed the exam, be sure you are given the appropriate paperwork:

- The CSCE, signed by all three examiners.
- Make sure the temporary identifier is filled in so you can use it to immediately go on the air with your new General Class frequency privileges.

Also, while you are waiting for your exam results, the VET may ask you to complete your Form 610, the application for your upgrade.

COMPLETING FCC FORM 610

FCC Form 610, the *Application for Amateur Operator/Primary Station License,* was revised in September, 1997, and the new form must be used on all amateur license applications. The new Form 610 contains a statement certifying that you have read and understand the FCC RF safety guidelines. If you do use an old version, it will be returned without action and you will be required to re-file on a current form.

At the time this book was printed, the FCC proposed (but had not yet implemented) to replace Form 610 with a new, shorter Form 605 and Schedule C. Your VET will probably have copies of the current, correct FCC amateur radio application form for your license upgrade. However, you may wish to obtain a correct, current application form ahead of time by downloading one from the FCC's website: http://www.fcc.gov/formpage.html.

Your Portion

First, it is very important that you complete the application legibly. Doing so will save you a lot of grief anytime you upgrade.

The greatest cause of a rejected Form 610 is a change in the way your name, address, or age(!) is on record with the FCC. If your present license reads "Jack Hudson" and you submit your upgrade as "John Hudson," your application will be rejected. If you have changed your address, you must note this on your new Form 610.

How can a birthday change? I don't know how, either, but the most common error is putting down the current year as the year in which you were born. This will cause a rejected application.

Pull out your old license and study it carefully. If just one letter or one number is any different on your application, the computer will probably reject it. Since most upgrades are filed electronically, you must be absolutely accurate on your Form 610 for an upgrade, especially when it comes to your name, address, and birthday. Letter for letter, number for number, it must be exactly the same for your electronically processed application to go through.

Your Examiner's Portion

The VET that administered your General Class exam must complete the "Administering VE's Report" on the bottom of the Form 610 and certify your application. They may then file your application electronically with their VEC for processing by the FCC, and send in your Form 610 paperwork, as well.

Your Upgrade to General Class

You will receive your General Class upgrade grant within 3 to 10 days, and you should receive a paper copy of your General Class license in about 3 weeks. There are many online services that regularly post the FCC database with new application and new upgrade information.

When you pass your General Class written exam and code test, you will be issued a CSCE—Certificate of Successful Completion of Examination. This CSCE allows you to begin using your new privileges immediately. After your call sign, append the letters "AG" to indicate your upgrade is being processed by the FCC. As soon as you see your upgrade on the electronic database, or receive your new license, you can drop the "AG" at the end of your call sign.

GENERAL CLASS CALL SIGNS

The Federal Communications Commission has exhausted the availability of "Group C" Technician and General Class call signs that begin with the letter "N," a number, and three other letters (such as, N9ABC).

If you did not check the "Change Call Sign" box on your Form 610 application for upgrade, you will simply keep your current call sign. However, if you do check the "Change Call Sign" box, you will receive an entry-level "Group D" call sign as if you were a newly-licensed amateur. I suggest you don't check the "Change Call Sign" box and stay with your present call sign.

VANITY CALL SIGNS

General, Technician-Plus, Technician, and Novice Class operators may request a vanity call sign from Group D or Group C. However, since Group C call signs are completely used up, only Group D call signs are available. These call signs have two letters, a number, and three letters (such as KA5GMO).

You also may request a call sign that was previously assigned to you that may have expired years ago, as well as a call sign of a close relative or former holder who is now deceased. This call sign can be from any group.

At the time this book was printed, the fee for a vanity call sign was $50 for a 10-year period. The FCC proposed, but had not yet implemented, reducing this fee to $12.90. You can obtain the correct Vanity call sign application forms on the FCC internet site: http://www.fcc.gov/wtb/amateur.

You can file the forms electronically, and then mail them with your check attached. Mail the required paperwork and fee to: FCC, PO Box 358994, Pittsburgh, PA 15251-5994. The hard copies and the fee must be received within 10 days of electronically filing or your application will be dismissed. See page 123 for more information.

As for your author, he's, staying with his original-issue WB6NOA call sign. If he changed it, he would be breaking a 30-year tradition!

CONGRATULATIONS! YOU PASSED!

After you pass the written examination and code test, congratulations are in order and we offer you a big welcome to the worldwide privileges of General Class! Day or night, summer or fall, sunshine or rain, there is always a worldwide band open and ready for General Class voice, code, PACTOR, and television communications. Your new worldwide privileges are added to your existing VHF and UHF privileges.

Before your go on the air, do a lot of listening. This will assure that you get started on the right foot with your new privileges. Remember, even the worldwide bands have band plans, so make sure you are operating within the plan for your worldwide communications.

I also would like you to write me so I can send you an exclusive General Class passing certificate, plus some valuable manufacturers' discount coupons. Send a self-addressed large envelope with 10 first class stamps loose on the inside to: Gordon West, WB6NOA, Radio School, Inc., 2414 College Drive, Costa Mesa, CA 92626.

SUMMARY

Once you have your General Class license, why not set your sights on the Advanced Class license? It's the next step up the ladder. While you will not gain any additional bands, you will get a little more elbow room on the voice portion of each worldwide band. The ultimate step, of course, is to go for your Extra Class license, which will give you full access to all amateur bands.

Advanced Class and *Extra Class* are books authored by Gordon West that will help you prepare for — and pass — those examinations and gain even greater privileges. If you can't find copies, call the W5YI Group at 800/669-9594, or check their web site: http://www.w5yi.org.

Welcome to worldwide amateur service operation. You are now part of a select group of more than 125,000 Americans who hold a General Class license!

Happy DX-ing!

Appendix

U.S. VOLUNTEER EXAMINER COORDINATORS IN THE AMATEUR SERVICE

Anchorage Amateur Radio Club
2628 Turnagain Parkway
Anchorage, AK 99517-1128
(907) 243-2221 [night]
(907) 343-8121 [day]

ARRL/VEC
225 Main Street
Newington, CT 06111-1494
VEC direct (860) 594-0300
FAX   (860) 594-0259
e-mail: vec@arrl.org

Central Alabama VEC, Inc.
1215 Dale Drive SE
Huntsville, AL 35801-2031
(205) 536-3904
FAX (205) 534-5557
e-mail: dtunstil@advicom.net

Golden Empire Amateur Radio Society
P.O. Box 508
Chico, CA 95927-0508
(916) 342-1180

Greater Los Angeles Amateur Radio
   Group
9737 Noble Avenue
North Hills, CA 91343-2403
(818) 892-2068
FAX (818) 892-9855
e-mail: glarg@ibm.net

Jefferson Amateur Radio Club
P.O. Box 24368
New Orleans, LA 70184-4368
(504) 832-6803
e-mail: dje01@gnofn.org

Laurel Amateur Radio Club, Inc.
P.O. Box 3039
Laurel, MD 20709-0039
(301) 572-5124 (1800-2100 hours)
(301) 317-7819
e-mail: rbusch@erols.com

Milwaukee Radio Amateurs Club, Inc.
P.O. Box 25707
Milwaukee, WI 53225
(414) 466-4267
FAX (414) 461-7730
e-mail: lesw9ycv@aol.com

MO-KAN/VEC
P.O. Box 11
Liberty, MO 64069-0011
(816) 781-7313
e-mail: wa0kuh@juno.com

Mountain Amateur Radio Club
P.O. Box 10
Burlington, WV 26710-0010
(304) 289-3576

Sandarc-VEC
P.O. Box 2446
La Mesa, CA 91943-2446
(619) 465-3926
FAX (619) 461-9515
e-mail: ws6f@juno.com

Sunnyvale VEC Amateur Radio Club, Inc.
P.O. Box 60307
Sunnyvale, CA 94088-0307
(408) 255-9000 (24 hours)
FAX (408) 366-8000
e-mail: vec@amateur-radio.org

Volunteer Examiners Club of America,
   W4VEC
3504 Stonehurst Place
High Point, NC 27265-2106
(910) 841-7576
FAX (910) 841-7503 (6th ring)
e-mail: w4vec@aol.com

Western Carolina Amateur Radio Society
   VEC, Inc.
5833 Clinton Hwy, Suite 203
Knoxville, TN 37912-2500
(423) 688-7771
FAX (423) 281-9481
e-mail: wcars@korrnet.org

W5YI-VEC
P.O. Box 565101
Dallas, TX 75356-5101
(817) 461-6443
FAX (817) 548-9594
e-mail: w5yi@internetmci.com

AMATEUR RADIO CALL SIGNS

As an aid to enforcement of the radio rules, transmitting stations throughout the world are required to identify themselves at intervals when they are in operation. In the U.S., amateur operators must identify their stations at least once every ten minutes and at the end of the communications exchange. By international agreement, the prefix letters of a station's call sign indicates the country in which that station is authorized to operate. On the DX airwaves, hams can readily identify the national origin of the ham signal they hear by its call sign prefix.

The national prefixes allocated to the United States are AA through AL, KA through KZ, NA through NZ, and WA through WZ. In addition, U.S. amateur station call signs include a number indicating U.S. geographic area. The map on the following page shows these geographic areas. The number is followed by suffix letters that indicate a specific amateur station.

The Amateur Operator/Primary Station call sign is issued by the FCC's licensing facility in Gettysburg, Pennsylvania, on a systematic basis after it receives your application information from the VEC. There are four call sign groupings, A, B, C and D. Tables showing the call sign groups and formats for operator/station licenses within and outside of the contiguous United States are shown on page 123.

- Group A call signs are issued to Extra Class licensees, and have a 1-by-2, 2-by-1, or 2-by-2 format. W9MU is an example.
- Group B call signs are issued to Advanced Class licensees, and have a 2-by-2 format. WA6PT is an example.
- Group C call signs are issued to General, Technician-Plus, and Technician Class licensees, and have a 1-by-3 format. N7LAT is an example. (However, because of the large number of Technician no-code licenses that have been issued, there are no remaining Group C licenses available. Thus, in accordance with FCC rules, new General, Technician-Plus, and Technician Class operators are issued Group D licenses.)
- Group D call signs are issued to Novice Class licensees, and have a 2-by-3 format. WA3ABC is an example.

Once assigned, a call sign is never changed unless the licensee specifically requests the change—even if they move out of the contiguous United States. FCC licensees residing in foreign countries must show a U.S. mailing address on their applications. You may change your call sign to a new group when you upgrade your Amateur Radio operator license.

Call Signs for Upgrades

The current automated Amateur Radio call sign assignment system has been in effect since 1978. It allows amateurs to obtain shorter and, theoretically, more desirable call signs in exchange for upgrading one's license.

The FCC authorizes amateurs who have already received their first license to immediately begin using their new privileges on the air when they upgrade. You must identify your call sign with a special identifier whenever operating outside the privileges of the license currently in your possession. This notifies those listening (including FCC monitoring stations) that you have recently upgraded and are authorized on new spectrum. Novices upgrading to Technician should append their call sign with the letters "KT," e.g., KB5AAA would add "temporary KT" to his/her call sign. You would use a slant bar when operating using Morse code. New General Class amateurs append their call signs with

"AG", Advanced "AA," and Extra Class "AE." There is no identifier applying to the Tech-Plus Class.

If Novices and Technicians who upgrade request a new call sign, they will receive a new 2-by-3 call sign, since all 1-by-3 "N" call signs have been assigned. Newly upgraded Advanced and Extra Class amateurs may request new Group B and A call sign formats. You may change your call sign to the next available call sign within your present group any time you wish by submitting

Call Sign Area for U.S. Geographical Areas

U.S. Call Sign Areas

Call Sign Area No.	Geographical Area
1	Maine, New Hampshire, Vermont, Massachusetts, Rhode Island, Connecticut
2	New York, New Jersey, Guam and the U. S. Virgin Islands
3	Pennsylvania, Delaware, Maryland, District of Columbia
4	Virginia, North and South Carolina, Georgia, Florida, Alabama, Tennessee, Kentucky, Midway Island, Puerto Rico[1]
5	Mississippi, Louisiana, Arkansas, Oklahoma, Texas, New Mexico
6	California, Hawaii[2]
7	Oregon, Washington, Idaho, Montana, Wyoming, Arizona, Nevada, Utah, Alaska[3]
8	Michigan, Ohio, West Virginia, American Samoa
9	Wisconsin, Illinois, Indiana
0	Colorado, Nebraska, North and South Dakota, Kansas, Minnesota, Iowa, Missouri, Northern Mariana Island

[1] Puerto Rico also issued Area #3. [2] Hawaii also issued Area #7. [3] Alaska also issued Areas #1 through #0.

an *Application Form 610 for Amateur Operator/Primary Station License.* Be sure to check line 4E and initial. Send to the FCC, 1270 Fairfield Road, Gettysburg, PA 17325-7245.

Vanity Call Sign System

In 1996, the FCC implemented a vanity call sign system allowing amateurs to request a station call sign of their choice. The cost of a vanity call sign is $50.00—payable by check or credit card to the FCC. At the time this book was printed, the FCC was considering reducing this fee to $12.90.

Amateur operators apply for a vanity call sign by submitting an FCC Form 610-V listing up to 25 call signs in order of preference to: FCC, Amateur Vanity Call Sign Requests, P.O. Box 358924, Pittsburgh, PA 15251-5924.

Amateur Call Sign Groups, Contiguous U.S.A.

Group	Format	Prefix Letters	Issued to
Group D	**2-by-3**	KA to KZ, WA to WZ	**Novice**
Group C	**1-by-3**	N*	**Technician/General**
Group B	**2-by-2**	KA to KZ, NA to NZ, WA to WZ	**Advanced Class**
Group A	**1-by-2**	K, N, W	**Extra Class**
	2-by-1	AA to AL, KA to KZ, NA to NZ, WA to WZ	**Extra Class**
	2-by-2	AA to AG, AI, AJ or AK	**Extra Class**

*W and K prefixes available under vanity call sign system.

Amateur Call Sign Groups, Non-Contiguous U.S.A.

Region 11 = Alaska
Region 12 = Caribbean Area including Puerto Rico
Region 13 = Pacific Area including Hawaii

Group	Format	Call Sign	Issued to
Group D	**2-by-3**		**Novice Class**
Region 11		Prefix KL or WL, area digit and three letter suffix	
Region 12		Prefix KP or WP, area digit and three letter suffix	
Region 13		Prefix KH or WH, area digit and three letter suffix	
Group C	**2-by-2**		**Technician/ General**
Region 11		Prefix KL, NL or WL, area digit and two letter suffix	
Region 12		Prefix NP or WP, area digit and two letter suffix	
Region 13		Prefix KH, NH or WH, area digit and two letter suffix	
Group B	**2-by-2**		**Advanced Class**
Region 11		Prefix AL, area digit and two letter suffix	
Region 12		Prefix KP, area digit and two letter suffix	
Region 13		Prefix AH, area digit and two letter suffix	
Group A	**2-by-1**		**Extra Class**
Region 11		Prefix AL, KL, NL or WL, area digit and one letter suffix	
Region 12		Prefix KP, NP, or WP, area digit and one letter suffix	
Region 13		Prefix AH, KH, NH or WH, area digit and one letter suffix	

It is also possible to apply for a vanity call sign online by accessing the FCC's World Wide Web site at: http://fcc.gov. (To reach the right file, select (1.) Electronic Filing, and (2.) Amateur Vanity Call Sign Application.)

You will keep your original call sign (and receive a refund, if requested) if none of the call signs you requested are available.

It is generally the goal of every amateur to obtain a call sign which is personal in some way. You are not allowed to choose a vanity call sign until you have received a sequential call sign from the FCC.

Special Event Call Sign System

Any licensed radio amateur may request a 1-by-1 station call sign to commemorate a special event. The call sign may be used for a period not to exceed 15 days. The 1-by-1 call sign must consist of the prefix letter K, N or W, a numeral 1 through 0, and a suffix letter. K5A is an example. The call sign is selected from a list of call signs shown on the common data base which is coordinated, maintained, and disseminated by the Special Events Call Sign Coordinators. The data base and instructions may be found at the following web site: http://ncvec.spindle.net.

ANTENNA ELEMENT EQUATIONS

Use the following equations to calculate the length of the driven, reflector and director elements of the respective antenna types as indicated.

Question	Equation
Cubical Quad Antenna	
G9B01, 02	Driven Element (each side in feet) $= \dfrac{1005}{f \text{ in MHz}} \div 4$
G9B03	Reflector Element (each side in feet) $= \dfrac{1030}{f \text{ in MHz}} \div 4$
Delta Loop Antenna Symmetrical	
G9B04, 05	Driven Element (each leg in feet) $= \dfrac{1005}{f \text{ in MHz}} \div 3$
G9B06	Reflector Element (each leg in feet) $= \dfrac{1030}{f \text{ in MHz}} \div 3$
Yagi Antenna	
G9A02	Driven Element (in feet) $\left(\dfrac{\lambda}{2}\right) = \dfrac{472}{f \text{ in MHz}}$
G9A03	Director Element (shorter element in feet) $= \dfrac{458}{f \text{ in MHz}}$
G9A04	Reflector Element (longer element in feet) $= \dfrac{490}{f \text{ in MHz}}$

AUTHORIZED FREQUENCY BANDS – AMATEUR SERVICE
(for U.S. Amateur Stations operating from ITU-Region 2–North and South America)

Meters	Novice	Technician[1,2]	Technician Plus[2]	General	Advanced	Extra Class
160				1800-2000 kHz/All	1800-2000 kHz/All	1800-2000 kHz/All
80	3675-3725 kHz/CW		3675-3725 kHz/CW	3525-3750 kHz/CW 3850-4000 kHz/Ph	3525-3750 kHz/CW 3775-4000 kHz/Ph	3500-4000 kHz/CW 3750-4000 kHz/Ph
40	7100-7150 kHz/CW		7100-7150 kHz/CW	7025-7150 kHz/CW 7225-7300 kHz/Ph	7025-7300 kHz/CW 7150-7300 kHz/Ph	7000-7300 kHz/CW 7150-7300 kHz/Ph
30				10.1-10.15 MHz/CW	10.1-10.15 MHz/CW	10.1-10.15 MHz/CW
20				14.025-14.15 MHz/CW 14.225-14.35 MHz/Ph	14.025-14.15 MHz/CW 14.175-14.35 MHz/Ph	14.0-14.35 MHz/CW 14.15-14.35 MHz/Ph
17				18.068-18.11 MHz/CW 18.11-18.168 MHz/Ph	18.068-18.11 MHz/CW 18.11-18.168 MHz/Ph	18.068-18.11 MHz/CW 18.11-18.168 MHz/Ph
15	21.1-21.2 MHz/CW		21.1-21.2 MHz/CW	21.025-21.2 MHz/CW 21.3-21.45 MHz/Ph	21.025-21.2 MHz/CW 21.225-21.45 MHz/Ph	21.0-21.45 MHz/CW 21.2-21.45 MHz/Ph
12				24.89-24.99 MHz/CW 24.93-24.99 MHz/Ph	24.89-24.99 MHz/CW 24.93-24.99 MHz/Ph	24.89-24.99 MHz/CW 24.93-24.99 MHz/Ph
10	28.1-28.5 MHz/CW 28.3-28.5 MHz/Ph		28.1-28.5 MHz/CW 28.3-28.5 MHz/Ph	28.0-29.7 MHz/CW 28.3-29.7 MHz/Ph	28.0-29.7 MHz/CW 28.3-29.7 MHz/Ph	28.0-29.7 MHz/CW 28.3-29.7 MHz/Ph
6		50-54 MHz/CW 50.1-54 MHz/Ph	50-54 MHz/CW 50.1-54 MHz/Ph	50-54 MHz/CW 50.1-54 MHz/Ph	50-54 MHz/CW 50.1-54 MHz/Ph	50-54 MHz/CW 50.1-54 MHz/Ph
2		144-148 MHz/CW 144.1-148 MHz/All	144-148 MHz/CW 144.1-148 MHz/All	144-148 MHz/CW 144.1-148 MHz/All	144-148 MHz/CW 144.1-148 MHz/All	144-148 MHz/CW 144.1-148 MHz/All
1.25	[3]222-225 MHz/All	[4]222-225 MHz/All	222-225 MHz/All	222-225 MHz/All	222-225 MHz/All	222-225 MHz/All
0.70		420-450 MHz/All	420-450 MHz/All	420-450 MHz/All	420-450 MHz/All	420-450 MHz/All
0.33		902-928 MHz/All	902-928 MHz/All	902-928 MHz/All	902-928 MHz/All	902-928 MHz/All
0.23	1270-1295 MHz/All	1240-1300 MHz/All	1240-1300 MHz/All	1240-1300 MHz/All	1240-1300 MHz/All	1240-1300 MHz/All

[1]No-Code License   [2]Effective 2/14/91   [3]Effective 2/1/94   [4]219-220 MHz is authorized for point-to-point fixed digital message forwarding systems.

Note: Morse code (CW, A1A) may be used on any frequency allocated to the amateur service. Telephony emission (abbreviated Ph above) authorized on certain bands as indicated. Higher class licensees may use slow-scan television and facsimile emissions on the Phone bands; radio teletype/digital on the CW bands. All amateur modes and emissions are authorized above 144.1 MHz. In actual practice, the modes/emissions used are somewhat more complicated than shown above due to the existence of various band plans and "gentlemen's agreements" concerning where certain operations should take place.

ITU Regions

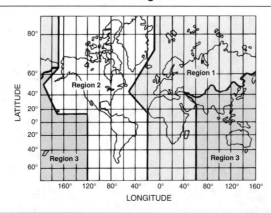

List of Countries Permitting Third-Party Traffic

Country	Call Sign Prefix	Country	Call Sign Prefix	Country	Call Sign Prefix
Antigua and Barbuda	V2	Ecuador	HC	Nicaragua	YN
Argentina	LU	El Salvador	YS	Panama	HP
Australia	VK	The Gambia	C5	Paraguay	ZP
Austria, Vienna	4U1VIC	Ghana	9G	Peru	OA
Belize	V3	Grenada	J3	Philippines	DU
Bolivia	CP	Guatemala	TG	St. Christopher & Nevis	V4
Bosnia-Herzegovina	T9	Guyana	8R	St. Lucia	J6
Brazil	PY	Haiti	HH	St. Vincent & Grenadines	J8
Canada	VE, VO, VY	Honduras	HR	Sierra Leone	9L
Chile	CE	Israel	4X	Swaziland	3D6
Colombia	HK	Jamaica	6Y	Trinidad and Tobago	9Y
Comoros	D6	Jordan	JY	United Kingdom	GB*
Costa Rica	TI	Liberia	EL	Uruguay	CX
Cuba	CO	Marshall Is.	V6	Venezuela	YV
Dominica	J7	Mexico	XE	ITU-Geneva	4U1ITU
Dominican Republic	HI	Micronesia	V6	VIC-Vienna	4U1VIC

*GB3 excluded

Countries Holding U.S. Reciprocal Agreements

Antigua, Barbuda	Chile	Greece	Liberia	Seychelles
Argentina	Colombia	Greenland	Luxembourg	Sierra Leone
Australia	Costa Rica	Grenada	Macedonia	Solomon Islands
Austria	Croatia	Guatemala	Marshall Is.	South Africa
Bahamas	Cyprus	Guyana	Mexico	Spain
Barbados	Denmark	Haiti	Micronesia	St. Lucia
Belgium	Dominica	Honduras	Monaco	St. Vincent and
Belize	Dominican Rep.	Iceland	Netherlands	Grenadines
Bolivia	Ecuador	India	Netherlands Ant.	Surinam
Bosnia-	El Salvador	Indonesia	New Zealand	Sweden
Herzegovina	Fiji	Ireland	Nicaragua	Switzerland
Botswana	Finland	Israel	Norway	Thailand
Brazil	France[2]	Italy	Panama	Trinidad, Tobago
Canada[1]	Germany	Jamaica	Paraguay	Tuvalu
		Japan	Papua New Guinea	United Kingdom[3]
		Jordan	Peru	Uruguay
		Kiribati	Philippines	Venezuela
		Kuwait	Portugal	

1. Do not need reciprocal permit.
2. Includes all French Territories
3. Includes all British Territories

POPULAR Q SIGNALS

Given below are a number of Q signals whose meanings most often need to be expressed with brevity and clarity in amateur work. (Q abbreviations take the form of questions only when each is sent followed by a question mark.)

QRA The name of my station is _____ .

QRG Will you tell me my exact frequency (or that of _____)? Your exact frequency (or that of _____) is _____ kHz.

QRH Does my frequency vary? Your frequency varies.

QRI How is the tone of my transmission? The tone of your transmission is _____ (1. Good; 2. Variable; 3. Bad).

QRJ Are you receiving me badly? I cannot receive you. Your signals are too weak.

QRK What is the intelligibility of my signals (or those of _____)? The intelligibility of your signals (or those of _____) is _____ (1. Bad; 2. Poor; 3. Fair; 4. Good; 5. Excellent).

QRL Are you busy? I am busy (or I am busy with _____). Please do not interfere.

QRM Is my transmission being interfered with? Your transmission is being interfered with _____ (1. Nil; 2. Slightly; 3. Moderately; 4. Severely; 5. Extremely).

QRN Are you troubled by static? I am troubled by static _____ (1-5 as under QRM).

QRO Shall I increase power? Increase power.

QRP Shall I decrease power? Decrease power.

QRQ Shall I send faster? Send faster (_____ WPM).

QRS Shall I send more slowly? Send more slowly (_____ WPM).

QRT Shall I stop sending? Stop sending.

QRU Have you anything for me? I have nothing for you.

QRV Are you ready? I am ready.

QRW Shall I inform _____ that you are calling on _____ kHz? Please inform _____ that I am calling on _____ kHz.

QRX When will you call me again? I will call you again at _____ hours (on _____ kHz).

QRY What is my turn? Your turn is numbered _____ .

QRZ Who is calling me? You are being called by _____ (on _____ kHz).

QSA What is the strength of my signals (or those of _____)? The strength of your signals (or those of _____) is _____ (1. Scarcely perceptible; 2. Weak; 3. Fairly good; 4. Good; 5. Very good).

QSB Are my signals fading? Your signals are fading.

QSD Is my keying defective? Your keying is defective.

QSG Shall I send _____ messages at a time? Send _____ messages at a time.

QSK Can you hear me between your signals and if so can I break in on your transmission? I can hear you between my signals; break in on my transmission.

QSL Can you acknowledge receipt? I am acknowledging receipt.

QSM Shall I repeat the last message which I sent you, or some previous message? Repeat the last message which you sent me [or message(s) number(s) _____].

QSN Did you hear me (or _____) on _____ kHz? I heard you (or _____) on _____ kHz.

QSO Can you communicate with _____ direct or by relay? I can communicate with _____ direct (or by relay through _____).

QSP Will you relay to _____ ? I will relay to _____ .

QST General call preceding a message addressed to all amateurs and ARRL members. This is in effect "CQ ARRL."

QSU Shall I send or reply on this frequency (or on _____ kHz)?

QSW Will you send on this frequency (or on _____ kHz)? I am going to send on this frequency (or on _____ kHz).

QSX Will you listen to _____ on _____ kHz? I am listening to _____ on _____ kHz.

QSY Shall I change to transmission on another frequency? Change to transmission on another frequency (or on _____ kHz).

QSZ Shall I send each word or group more than once? Send each word or group twice (or _____ times).

QTA Shall I cancel message number _____ ? Cancel message number _____ .

QTB Do you agree with my counting of words? I do not agree with your counting of words. I will repeat the first letter or digit of each word or group.

QTC How many messages have you to send? I have messages for you (or for _____).
QTH What is your location? My location is _____.
QTR What is the correct time? The time is _____.

Source: ARRL

COMMON CW ABBREVIATIONS

AA	All after		**NW**	Now; I resume transmission
AB	All before		**OB**	Old boy
ABT	About		**OM**	Old man
ADR	Address		**OP-OPR**	Operator
AGN	Again		**OT**	Old timer; old top
ANT	Antenna		**PBL**	Preable
BCI	Broadcast interference		**PSE-PLS**	Please
BK	Break; break me; break in		**PWR**	Power
BN	All between; been		**PX**	Press
B4	Before		**R**	Received as transmitted; are
C	Yes			
CFM	Confirm; I confirm		**RCD**	Received
CK	Check		**REF**	Refer to; referring to; reference
CL	I am closing my station; call			
CLD-CLG	Called; calling		**RPT**	Repeat; I repeat
CUD	Could		**SED**	Said
CUL	See you later		**SEZ**	Says
CUM	Come		**SIG**	Signature; signal
CW	Continuous Wave		**SKED**	Schedule
DLD-DLVD	Delivered		**SRI**	Sorry
DX	Distance		**SVC**	Service; prefix to service message
FB	Fine business; excellent			
GA	Go ahead (or resume sending)		**TFC**	Traffic
			TMW	Tomorrow
GB	Good-by		**TNX**	Thanks
GBA	Give better address		**TU**	Thank you
GE	Good evening		**TVI**	Television interference
GG	Going		**TXT**	Text
GM	Good morning		**UR-URS**	Your; you're; yours
GN	Good night		**VFO-**	Variable-frequency oscillator
GND	Ground		**VY**	Very
GUD	Good		**WA**	Word after
HI	The telegraphic laugh; high		**WB**	Word before
HR	Here; hear		**WD-WDS**	Word; words
HV	Have		**WKD-WKG**	Worked; working
HW	How		**WL**	Well; will
LID	A poor operator		**WUD**	Would
MILS	Milliamperes		**WX**	Weather
MSG	Message; prefix to radio-gram		**XMTR**	Transmitter
			XTAL	Crystal
N	No		**XYL**	Wife
ND	Nothing doing		**YL**	Young lady
NIL	Nothing; I have nothing for you		**73**	Best regards
			88	Love and kisses
NR	Number			

EMISSION TYPE DESIGNATORS – AMATEUR RADIO SERVICE

First Symbol–Modulation system

A = Double sideband AM, C = Vestigial sideband AM, D = Amplitude/angle modulated, F = Frequency modulation, G = Phase modulation, H = Single sideband/full carrier, J = Single sideband/suppressed carrier, K = AM pulse, L = Pulse modulated in width/duration, M = Pulse modulated in position/phase, P = Unmodulated pulses, Q = Angle modulated during pulse, V = Combination of pulse emissions, W = Other types of pulses, R = Single sideband/reduced or variable level carrier.

Second Symbol–Nature of signal modulating carrier

0 = No modulation, 1 = Digital data without modulated subcarrier, 2 = Digital data on modulated subcarrier, 3 = Analog modulated, 7 = Two or more channels of digital data, 8 = Two or more channels of analog data, 9 = Combination of analog and digital information, X = Other

Third Symbol–Information to be conveyed

A = Manually received telegraphy, B = Automatically received telegraphy, C = Facsimile (FAX), D = Digital information, E = Voice telephony, F = Video/television, N = No information, W = Combination of these, X = Other.

1. **CW** - International Morse code telegraphy emissions having designators with A, C, H, J or R as the first symbol, 1 as the second symbol, A or B as the third symbol, and emissions J2A and J2B.

2. **DATA** - Telemetry, telecommand and computer communications emissions having designators with A, C, D, F, G, H, J or R as the first symbol: 1 as the second symbol; D as the third symbol; and also emission J2D. Only a digital code of a type specifically authorized in in this Part may be transmitted.

3. **IMAGE** - Facsimile and television emissions having designators with A, C, D, F, G, H, J or R as the first symbol; 1, 2 or 3 as the second symbol; C or F as the third symbol; and also emissions having B as the first symbol; 7, 8 or 9 as the second symbol; W as the third symbol.

4. **MCW (Modulated carrier wave)** - Tone-modulated international Morse code telegraphy emissions having designators with A, C, D, F, G, H or R as the first symbol; 2 as the second symbol; A or B as the third symbol.

5. **PHONE** - Speech and other sound emissions having designators with A, C, D, F, G, H, J or R as the first symbol; 1, 2 or 3 as the second symbol; E as the third symbol. Also speech emissions having B as the first symbol; 7, 8 or 9 as the second symbol; E as the third symbol. MCW for the purpose of performing the station identification procedure, or for providing telegraphy practice interspersed with speech, or incidental tones for the purpose of selective calling, or alerting or to control the level of a demodulated signal may also be considered phone.

6. **PULSE** - Emissions having designators with K, L, M, P, Q, V or W as the first symbol; 0, 1, 2, 3, 7, 8, 9 or X as the second symbol; A, B, C, D, E, F, N, W or X as the third symbol.

7. **RTTY (Radioteletype)** - Narrow-band, direct-printing telegraphy emissions having designators with A, C, D, F, G, H, J or R as the first symbol; 1 as the second symbol; B as the third symbol; and also emission J2B. Only a digital code of a type specifically authorized in the §Part 97.3 rules may be transmitted.

8. **SS (Spread Spectrum)** - Emissions using bandwidth-expansion modulation emissions having designators with A, C, D, F, G, H, J or R as the first symbol; X as the second symbol; X as the third symbol. Only a SS emission of a type specifically authorized in §Part 97.3 rules may be transmitted.

9. **TEST** - Emissions containing no information having the designators with N as the third symbol. Test does not include pulse emissions with no information or modulation unless pulse emissions are also authorized in the frequency band.

b. Back

a. Front

Form 610 Novice and Technician Class License Application Form
Front must be filled out per attached. No entries on back unless handicapped.

The W5YI RF Safety Tables

(Developed by Fred Maia, W5YI Group, working in cooperation with the ARRL.)

There are two ways to determine whether your station's radio frequency signal radiation is within the MPE (Maximum Permissible Exposure) guidelines established by the FCC for *"controlled"* and *"uncontrolled"* environments. One way is direct *"measurement"* of the RF fields. The second way is through *"prediction"* using various antenna modeling, equations and calculation methods described in the FCC's *OET Bulletin 65* and *Supplement B.*

In general, most amateurs will not have access to the appropriate calibrated equipment to make precise field strength/power density measurements. The field-strength meters in common use by amateur operators and inexpensive, hand-held field strength meters do not provide the accuracy necessary for reliable measurements, especially when different frequencies may be encountered at a given measurement location. It is more practical for amateurs to determine their PEP output power at the antenna and then look up the required distances to the controlled/uncontrolled environments using the following tables, which were developed using the prediction equations supplied by the FCC.

The FCC has determined that radio operators and their families are in the "controlled" environment and your neighbors and passers-by are in the "uncontrolled" environment. The estimated minimum compliance distances are in meters from the transmitting antenna to either the occupational/controlled exposure environment ("Con") or the general population/uncontrolled exposure environment ("Unc") using typical antenna gains for the amateur service and assuming 100% duty cycle and maximum surface reflection. Therefore, these charts represent the worst case scenario. They do not take into consideration compliance distance reductions that would be caused by:

(1) Feed line losses, which reduce power output at the antenna especially at the VHF and higher frequency levels.

(2) Duty cycle caused by the emission type. The emission type factor accounts for the fact that, for some modulated emission types that have a non-constant envelope, the PEP can be considerably larger than the average power. Multiply the above distances by 0.4 if you are using CW Morse telegraphy and 0.2 for two-way SSB (single sideband) voice. There is no reduction for FM.

(3) Duty cycle caused by on/off time or "time-averaging." The RF safety guidelines permit RF exposures to be averaged over certain periods of time with the average not to exceed the limit for continuous exposure. The averaging time for occupational/controlled exposures is six minutes, while the averaging time for general population/uncontrolled exposures is 30 minutes. For example, if the relevant time interval for time-averaging is six minutes, an amateur could be exposed to two times the applicable power density limit for three minutes as long as he or she were not exposed at all for the preceding or following three minutes.

A routine evaluation is not required for vehicular mobile or hand-held transceiver stations. Amateur Radio operators should be aware, however, of the potential for exposure to RF electromagnetic fields from these stations, and take measures (such as reducing transmitting power to the minimum necessary, positioning the radiating antenna as far from humans as practical, and limiting continuous transmitting time) to protect themselves and the occupants of their vehicles.

Amateur Radio operators should also be aware that the new FCC radio-frequency safety regulations address exposure to people—and not the strength of the signal. Amateurs may exceed the Maximum Permissible Exposure (MPE) limits as long as no one is exposed to the radiation.

How to read the chart: If you are radiating 500 watts from your 10 meter dipole (about a 3 dB gain), there must be at least 4.5 meters (about 15 feet) between you (and your family) and the antenna—and a distance of 10 meters (about 33 feet) between the antenna and your neighbors.

Medium and High Frequency Amateur Bands
All distances are in meters

Freq. (MF/HF) (MHz/Band)	Antenna Gain (dBi)	Peak Envelope Power (watts)							
		100 watts		500 watts		1000 watts		1500 watts	
		Con.	Unc.	Con.	Unc	Con.	Unc.	Con.	Unc.
2.0 (160m)	0	0.1	0.2	0.3	0.5	0.5	0.7	0.6	0.8
2.0 (160m)	3	0.2	0.3	0.5	0.7	0.6	1.06	0.8	1.2
4.0 (75/80m)	0	0.2	0.4	0.4	1.0	0.6	1.3	0.7	1.6
4.0 (75/80m)	3	0.3	0.6	0.6	1.3	0.9	1.9	1.0	2.3
7.3 (40m)	0	0.3	0.8	0.8	1.7	1.1	2.5	1.3	3.0
7.3 (40m)	3	0.5	1.1	1.1	2.5	1.6	3.5	1.9	4.2
7.3 (40m)	6	0.7	1.5	1.5	3.5	2.2	4.9	2.7	6.0
10.15 (30m)	0	0.5	1.1	1.1	2.4	1.5	3.4	1.9	4.2
10.15 (30m)	3	0.7	1.5	1.5	3.4	2.2	4.8	2.6	5.9
10.15 (30m)	6	1.0	2.2	2.2	4.8	3.0	6.8	3.7	8.3
14.35 (20m)	0	0.7	1.5	1.5	3.4	2.2	4.8	2.6	5.9
14.35 (20m)	3	1.0	2.2	2.2	4.8	3.0	6.8	3.7	8.4
14.35 (20m)	6	1.4	3.0	3.0	6.8	4.3	9.6	5.3	11.8
14.35 (20m)	9	1.9	4.3	4.3	9.6	6.1	13.6	7.5	16.7
18.168 (17m)	0	0.9	1.9	1.9	4.3	2.7	6.1	3.3	7.5
18.168 (17m)	3	1.2	2.7	2.7	6.1	3.9	8.6	4.7	10.6
18.168 (17m)	6	1.7	3.9	3.9	8.6	5.5	12.2	6.7	14.9
18.168 (17m)	9	2.4	5.4	5.4	12.2	7.7	17.2	9.4	21.1
21.145 (15m)	0	1.0	2.3	2.3	5.1	3.2	7.2	4.0	8.8
21.145 (15m)	3	1.4	3.2	3.2	7.2	4.6	10.2	5.6	12.5
21.145 (15m)	6	2.0	4.6	4.6	10.2	6.4	14.4	7.9	17.6
21.145 (15m)	9	2.9	6.4	6.4	14.4	9.1	20.3	11.1	24.9
24.99 (12m)	0	1.2	2.7	2.7	5.9	3.8	8.4	4.6	10.3
24.99 (12m)	3	1.7	3.8	3.8	8.4	5.3	11.9	6.5	14.5
24.99 (12m)	6	2.4	5.3	5.3	11.9	7.5	16.8	9.2	20.5
24.99 (12m)	9	3.4	7.5	7.5	16.8	10.6	23.7	13.0	29.0
29.7 (10m)	0	1.4	3.2	3.2	7.1	4.5	10.0	5.5	12.2
29.7 (10m)	3	2.0	4.5	4.5	10.0	6.3	14.1	7.7	17.3
29.7 (10m)	6	2.8	6.3	6.3	14.1	8.9	19.9	10.9	24.4
29.7 (10m)	9	4.0	8.9	8.9	19.9	12.6	28.2	15.4	34.5

VHF/UHFAmateur Bands

All Distances are in Meters

Freq. (VHF/UHF) (MHz/Band)	Antenna Gain (dBi)	Peak Envelope Power (watts)							
		50 watts		100 watts		500 watts		1000 watts	
		Con.	Unc.	Con.	Unc	Con.	Unc.	Con.	Unc.
50 (6m)	0	1.0	2.3	1.4	3.2	3.2	7.1	4.5	10.1
50 (6m)	3	1.4	3.2	2.0	4.5	4.5	10.1	6.4	14.3
50 (6m)	6	2.0	4.5	2.8	6.4	6.4	14.2	9.0	20.1
50 (6m)	9	2.8	6.4	4.0	9.0	9.0	20.1	12.7	28.4
50 (6m)	12	4.0	9.0	5.7	12.7	12.7	28.4	18.0	40.2
50 (6m)	15	5.7	12.7	8.0	18.0	18.0	40.2	25.4	56.8
144 (2m)	0	1.0	2.3	1.4	3.2	3.2	7.1	4.5	10.1
144 (2m)	3	1.4	3.2	2.0	4.5	4.5	10.1	6.4	14.3
144 (2m)	6	2.0	4.5	2.8	6.4	6.4	14.2	9.0	20.1
144 (2m)	9	2.8	6.4	4.0	9.0	9.0	20.1	12.7	28.4
144 (2m)	12	4.0	9.0	5.7	12.7	12.7	28.4	18.0	40.2
144 (2m)	15	5.7	12.7	8.0	18.0	18.0	40.2	25.4	56.8
144 (2m)	20	10.1	22.6	14.3	32.0	32.0	71.4	45.1	101.0
222 (1.25m)	0	1.0	2.3	1.4	3.2	3.2	7.1	4.5	10.1
222 (1.25m)	3	1.4	3.2	2.0	4.5	4.5	10.1	6.4	14.3
222 (1.25m)	6	2.0	4.5	2.8	6.4	6.4	14.2	9.0	20.1
222 (1.25m)	9	2.8	6.4	4.0	9.0	9.0	20.1	12.7	28.4
222 (1.25m)	12	4.0	9.0	5.7	12.7	12.7	28.4	18.0	40.2
222 (1.25m)	15	5.7	12.7	8.0	18.0	18.0	40.2	25.4	56.8
450 (70cm)	0	0.8	1.8	1.2	2.6	2.6	5.8	3.7	8.2
450 (70cm)	3	1.2	2.6	1.6	3.7	3.7	8.2	5.2	11.6
450 (70cm)	6	1.6	3.7	2.3	5.2	5.2	11.6	7.4	16.4
450 (70cm)	9	2.3	5.2	3.3	7.3	7.3	16.4	10.4	23.2
450 (70cm)	12	3.3	7.3	4.6	10.4	10.4	23.2	14.7	32.8
902 (33cm)	0	0.6	1.3	0.8	1.8	1.8	4.1	2.6	5.8
902 (33cm)	3	0.8	1.8	1.2	2.6	2.6	5.8	3.7	8.2
902 (33cm)	6	1.2	2.6	1.6	3.7	3.7	8.2	5.2	11.6
902 (33cm)	9	1.6	3.7	2.3	5.2	5.2	11.6	7.3	16.4
902 (33cm)	12	2.3	5.2	3.3	7.3	7.3	16.4	10.4	23.2
1240 (23cm)	0	0.5	1.1	0.7	1.6	1.6	3.5	2.2	5.0
1240 (23cm)	3	0.7	1.6	1.0	2.2	2.2	5.0	3.1	7.0
1240 (23cm)	6	1.0	2.2	1.4	3.1	3.1	7.0	4.4	9.9
1240 (23cm)	9	1.4	3.1	2.0	4.4	4.4	9.9	6.3	14.0
1240 (23cm)	12	2.0	4.4	2.8	6.2	6.2	14.0	8.8	19.8

All distances are in meters. To convert from meters to feet multiply meters by 3.28. Distance indicated is shortest line-of-sight distance to point where MPE limit for appropriate exposure tier is predicted to occur.

Glossary

Advanced: An amateur operator who has passed Element 2, 3A, 3B, and 4A written theory examinations and Element 1A and 1B code tests to demonstrate Morse code proficiency to 13 wpm.

Amateur communication: Noncommercial radio communication by or among amateur stations solely with a personal aim and without personal or business interest.

Amateur operator/primary station license: An instrument of authorization issued by the FCC comprised of a station license, and also incorporating an operator license indicating the class of privileges.

Amateur operator: A person holding a valid license to operate an amateur station issued by the FCC. Amateur operators are frequently referred to as ham operators.

Amateur Radio services: The amateur service, the amateur-satellite service and the radio amateur civil emergency service.

Amateur-satellite service: A radiocommunication service using stations on Earth and satellites for the same purpose as those of the amateur service.

Amateur service: A radiocommunication service for the purpose of self-training, intercommunication and technical investigations carried out by amateurs; that is, duly authorized persons interested in radio technique solely with a personal aim and without pecuniary interest.

Amateur station: A station licensed in the amateur service embracing necessary apparatus at a particular location used for amateur communication.

AMSAT: Radio Amateur Satellite Corporation, a nonprofit scientific organization. (P.O. Box #27, Washington, DC 20044)

ANSI: American National Standards Institute. A nongovernment organization that develops recommended standards for a variety of applications.

Antenna gain: The increase as a result of the physical construction of the antenna which confines the radiation to desired or useful directions. Usually specified in dB, referenced to the gain of a dipole.

APRS: Automatic Position Radio System, which takes GPS (Global Positioning System) information and translates it into an automatic packet of digital information.

ARES: Amateur Radio Emergency Service—the emergency division of the American Radio Relay League. Also see RACES

ARRL: American Radio Relay League, national organization of U.S. Amateur Radio operators. (225 Main Street, Newington, CT 06111)

Audio Frequency (AF): The range of frequencies that can be heard by the human ear, generally 20 hertz to 20 kilohertz.

Automatic control: The use of devices and procedures for station control without the control operator being present at the control point when the station is transmitting.

Automatic Volume Control (AVC): A circuit that continually maintains a constant audio output volume in spite of deviations in input signal strength.

Beam or Yagi antenna: An antenna array that receives or transmits RF energy in a particular direction. Usually rotatable.

Block diagram: A simplified outline of an electronic system where circuits or components are shown as boxes.

Broadcasting: Information or programming transmitted by radio intended for the general public.

Bulletin No. 65: The Office of Engineering & Technology bulletin that provides specified safety guidelines for human exposure to radiofrequency (RF) radiation.

Business communications: Any transmission or communication the purpose of which is to facilitate the regular business or commercial affairs of any party. Business communications are prohibited in the amateur service.

Call Book: A published list of all licensed amateur operators available in North American and Foreign editions.

Call sign: The FCC systematically assigns each amateur station its primary call sign.

Carrier frequency: The frequency of an unmodulated electromagnetic wave, usually specified in kilohertz or megahertz.

Certificate of Successful Completion of Examination (CSCE): A certificate providing examination credit for 365 days. Both written and code credit can be authorized.

Coaxial cable, Coax: A concentric, two-conductor cable in which one conductor surrounds the other, separated by an insulator.

Controlled Environment: Involves people who are aware of and who can exercise control over radiofrequency exposure. Controlled exposure limits apply to both occupational workers and Amateur Radio operators and their immediate households.

Control operator: An amateur operator designated by the licensee of an amateur station to be responsible for the station transmissions.

Coordinated repeater station: An amateur repeater station for which the transmitting and receiving frequencies have been recommended by the recognized repeater coordinator.

Coordinated Universal Time (UTC): (Also Greenwich Mean Time, UCT or Zulu time.) The time at the zero-degree (0°) Meridian which passes through Greenwich, England. A universal time among all amateur operators.

Crystal: A quartz or similar material which has been ground to produce natural vibrations of a specific frequency. Quartz crystals produce a high degree of frequency stability in radio transmitters.

CW: See Morse code.

Dipole antenna: The most common wire antenna. Length is equal to one-half of the wavelength. Fed by coaxial cable.

Dummy antenna: A device or resistor which serves as a transmitter's antenna without radiating radio waves. Generally used to tune up a radio transmitter.

Duplex: Transmitting on one frequency, and receiving on another, commonly used in mobile telephone use, as well as mobile business radio on UHF frequencies.

Duplexer: A device that allows a single antenna to be simultaneously used for both reception and transmission.

Duty cycle: As applies to RF safety, the percentage of time that a transmitter is "on" versus "off" in a 6- or 30-minute time period.

Effective Radiated Power (ERP): The product of the transmitter (peak envelope) power, expressed in watts, delivered to the antenna, and the relative gain of an antenna over that of a half wave dipole antenna.

Electromagnetic radiation: The propagation of radiant energy, including infrared, visible light, ultraviolet, radiofrequency, gamma and x-rays, through space and matter.

Emergency communication: Any amateur communication directly relating to the immediate safety of life of individuals or the immediate protection of property.

Examination Element: The written theory examination and/or Morse code test prescribed by the FCC for various classes of Amateur Radio licenses. Generals must pass an Element 3B written exam and an Element 1B code test.

Extra: An amateur operator at the top class of the amateur service who has passed Element 2, 3A, 3B, 4A and 4B written theory examinations and an Element 1C code test (or 1A, 1B and 1C code tests) to demonstrate Morse code proficiency to 20 wpm.

Far Field: The electromagnetic field located at a great distance from a transmitting antenna. The far field begins at a distance that depends on many factors, including the wavelength and the size of the antenna. Radio signals are normally received in the far field.

FCC Form 610: The FCC application form used to apply for a new amateur operator/primary station license or to renew or modify an existing license.

Federal Communications Commission (FCC): A board of five Commissioners, appointed by the President, having the power to regulate wire and radio telecommunications in the U.S.

Feedline: A system of conductors that connects an antenna to a receiver or transmitter.

Field Day: Annual activity sponsored by the ARRL to demonstrate emergency preparedness of amateur operators.

Field strength: A measure of the intensity of an electric or magnetic field. Electric fields are measured in volts per meter; magnetic fields in amperes per meter.

Filter: A device used to block or reduce alternating currents or signals at certain frequencies while allowing others to pass unimpeded.

Frequency: The number of cycles of alternating current in one second.

Frequency coordinator: An individual or organization which recommends frequencies and other operating and/or technical parameters for amateur repeater operation in order to avoid or minimize potential interferences.

Frequency Modulation (FM): A method of varying a radio carrier wave by causing its frequency to vary in accordance with the information to be conveyed.

Frequency privileges: The transmitting frequency bands available to the various classes of amateur operators. The Novice and Technician Class privileges are listed in Part 97.301 of the FCC rules.

General: An amateur operator who has passed Element 2, 3A, and 3B written theory examinations and Element 1A and 1B code tests to demonstrate Morse code proficiency to 13 wpm.

Ground: A connection, accidental or intentional, between a device or circuit and the earth or some common body and the earth or some common body serving as the earth.

Ground wave: A radio wave that is propagated near or at the earth's surface.

Half-Duplex: A method of operation on a duplex (separate transmit, separate receive) frequency pair where the operator only receives when the microphone button is released. Half-duplex does not permit simultaneous talk and listen.

Handi-Ham system: Amateur organization dedicated to assisting handicapped amateur operators. (3915 Golden Valley Road, Golden Valley, MN 55422)

Harmful interference: Interference which seriously degrades, obstructs or repeatedly interrupts the operation of a radio communication service.

Harmonic: A radio wave that is a multiple of the fundamental frequency. The second harmonic is twice the fundamental frequency, the third harmonic, three times, etc.

Hertz: One complete alternating cycle per second. Named after Heinrich R. Hertz, a German physicist. The number of hertz is the frequency of the audio or radio wave.

High Frequency (HF): The band of frequencies that lie between 3 and 30 Megahertz. It is from these frequencies that radio waves are returned to earth from the ionosphere.

High-Pass filter: A device that allows passage of high frequency signals but attenuates the lower frequencies. When installed on a television set, a high-pass filter allows TV frequencies to pass while blocking lower frequency amateur signals.

Interference: The effect that occurs when two or more radio stations are transmitting at the same time. This includes undesired noise or other radio signals on the same frequency.

Inverse Square Law: The physical principle by which power density decreases as you get further away from a transmitting antenna. RF power density decreases by the inverse square of the distance.

Ionization: The process of adding or stripping away electrons from atoms or molecules. Ionization occurs when substances are heated at high temperatures or exposed to high voltages. It can lead to significant genetic damage in biological tissue.

Ionosphere: Outer limits of atmosphere from which HF amateur communications signals are returned to earth.

IRC: International Reply Coupon, a method of prepaying postage for a foreign amateur's QSL card.

Jamming: The intentional, malicious interference with another radio signal.

Key clicks, Chirps: Defective keying of a telegraphy signal sounding like tapping or high varying pitches.

Linear amplifier: A device that accurately reproduces a radio wave in magnified form.

Long wire: A horizontal wire antenna that is one wavelength or longer in length.

Low-Pass filter: Device connected to worldwide transmitters that inhibits passage of higher frequencies that cause television interference but does not affect amateur transmissions.

Machine: A ham slang word for an automatic repeater station.

Malicious interference: See jamming.

MARS: The Military Affiliate Radio System. An organization that coordinates the activities of amateur communications with military radio communications.

Maximum authorized transmitting power: Amateur stations must use no more than the maximum transmitter power necessary to carry out the desired communications. The maximum P.E.P. output power levels authorized Novices are 200 watts in the 80-, 40-, 15- and 10-meter bands, 25 watts in the 222-MHz band, and 5 watts in the 1270-MHz bands.

Maximum Permissible Exposure (MPE): The maximum amount of electric and magnetic RF energy to which a person may safely be exposed.

Maximum usable frequency (MUF): The highest frequency that will be returned to earth from the ionosphere.

Medium frequency (MF): The band of frequencies that lies between 300 and 3,000 kHz (3 MHz).

Microwave: Electromagnetic waves with a frequency of 300 MHz to 300 GHz. Microwaves can cause heating of biological tissue.

Mobile operation: Radio communications conducted while in motion or during halts at unspecified locations.

Mode: Type of transmission such as voice, teletype, code, television, facsimile.

Modulate: To vary the amplitude, frequency or phase of a radiofrequency wave in accordance with the information to be conveyed.

Morse code: International Morse code, A1A emission. Interrupted continuous wave communications using a dot-dash code for letters, numbers and operating procedure signs.

Near Field: The electromagnetic field located in the immediate vicinity of the antenna. Energy in the near field depends on the size of the antenna, its wavelength and transmission power.

No-Code Technician operator: An Amateur Radio operator who has successfully passed Element 2 and 3A.

Nonionizing radiation: Electromagnetic waves, or fields, which do not have the capability to alter the molecular structure of substances. RF energy is nonionizing radiation.

Novice operator: An FCC licensed, entry-level amateur operator in the amateur service.

Occupational exposure: See controlled environment.

OET: Office of Engineering & Technology, a branch of the FCC that has developed the guidelines for radiofrequency (RF) safety.

Ohm's law: The basic electrical law explaining the relationship between voltage, current and resistance. The current I in a circuit is equal to the voltage E divided by the resistance R, or $I = E/R$.

OSCAR: "Orbiting Satellite Carrying Amateur Radio." A series of satellites designed and built by amateur operators of several nations.

Oscillator: A device for generating oscillations or vibrations of an audio or radiofrequency signal.

Output power: The radiofrequency output power of a transmitter's final radiofrequency stage as measured at the output terminal while connected to a load of the impedance recommended by the manufacturer.

Packet radio: A digital method of communicating computer-to-computer. A terminal-node controller makes up the packet of data and directs it to another packet station.

Peak Envelope Power (PEP): 1. The power during one radiofrequency cycle at the crest of the modulation envelope, taken under normal operating conditions. 2. The maximum power that can be obtained from a transmitter.

Phone patch: Interconnection of amateur service to the public switched telephone network, and operated by the control operator of the station.

Power density: A measure of the strength of an electromagnetic field at a distance from its source. Usually expressed in milliwatts per square centimeter (mW/cm^2). Far-field power density decreases according to the Law of Inverse Squares.

Power supply: A device or circuit that provides the appropriate voltage and current to another device or circuit.

Propagation: The travel of electromagnetic waves or sound waves through a medium.

Public exposure: See "uncontrolled" environment.

Q-signals: International three-letter abbreviations beginning with the letter Q used primarily to convey information using the Morse code.

QSL Bureau: An office that bulk processes QSL (radio confirmation) cards for (or from) foreign amateur operators as a postage saving mechanism.

RACES (Radio Amateur Civil Emergency Service): A radio service using amateur stations for civil defense communications during periods of local, regional, or national emergencies.

Radiation: Electromagnetic energy, such as radio waves, traveling forth into space from a transmitter.

Radiofrequency (RF): The range of frequencies over 20 kilohertz that can be propagated through space.

Radiofrequency (RF) radiation: Electromagnetic fields or waves having a frequency between 3 kHz and 300 GHz.

Radiofrequency spectrum: The eight electromagnetic bands ranked according to their frequency and wavelength. Specifically, the very-low, low, medium, high, very-high, ultra-high, super-high, and extremely-high frequency bands.

Radio wave: A combination of electric and magnetic fields varying at a radiofrequency and traveling through space at the speed of light.

Repeater operation: Automatic amateur stations that retransmit the signals of other amateur stations.

Routine RF radiation evaluation: The process of determining if the RF energy from a transmitter exceeds the Maximum Permissible Exposure (MPE) limits in a controlled or uncontrolled environment.

RST Report: A telegraphy signal report system of Readability, Strength and Tone.

S-meter: A voltmeter calibrated from 0 to 9 that indicates the relative signal strength of an incoming signal at a radio receiver.

Selectivity: The ability of a circuit (or radio receiver) to separate the desired signal from those not wanted.

Sensitivity: The ability of a circuit (or radio receiver) to detect a specified input signal.

Short circuit: An unintended, low-resistance connection across a voltage source resulting in high current and possible damage.

Shortwave: The high frequencies that lie between 3 and 30 Megahertz that are propagated long distances.

Simplex: A method of operation of a communication circuit which can receive or transmit, but not both simultaneously. Thus, system stations are operating on the same transmit and receive frequency.

Single-Sideband (SSB): A method of radio transmission in which the RF carrier and one of the sidebands is suppressed and all of the information is carried in the one remaining sideband.

Skip wave, Skip zone: A radio wave reflected back to earth. The distance between the radio transmitter and the site of a radio wave's return to earth.

Sky-wave: A radio wave that is reflected back to earth. Sometimes called an ionospheric wave.

Specific Absorption Rate (SAR): The time rate at which radiofrequency energy is absorbed into the human body.

Spectrum: A series of radiated energies arranged in order of wavelength. The radio spectrum extends from 20 kilohertz upward.

Spurious Emissions: Unwanted radiofrequency signals emitted from a transmitter that sometimes cause interference.

Station license, location: No transmitting station shall be operated in the amateur service without being licensed by the FCC. Each amateur station shall have one land location, the address of which appears in the station license.

Sunspot Cycle: An 11-year cycle of solar disturbances which greatly affects radio wave propagation.

Technician: A no-code amateur operator.

Technician-Plus: An amateur operator who has passed a 5-wpm code test in addition to Technician Class requirements.

Telegraphy: Communications transmission and reception using CW, International Morse code.

Telephony: Communications transmission and reception in the voice mode.

Telecommunications: The electrical conversion, switching, transmission and control of audio video and data signals by wire or radio.

Temporary operating authority: Authority to operate your amateur station while awaiting arrival of an upgraded license.

Terrestrial station location: Any location of a radio station on the surface of the earth including the sea.

Thermal effects: As applies to RF radiation, biological tissue damage resulting because of the body's inability to cope with or dissipate excessive heat.

Third-party traffic: Amateur communication by or under the supervision of the control operator at an amateur station to another amateur station on behalf of others.

Time-averaging: As applies to RF safety, the amount of electromagnetic radiation over a given time. The premise of time-averaging is that the human body can tolerate the thermal load caused by high, localized RF exposures for short periods of time.

Transceiver: A combination radio transmitter and receiver.

Transition region: Area where power density decreases inversely with distance from the antenna.

Transmatch: An antenna tuner used to match the impedance of the transmitter output to the transmission line of an antenna.

Transmitter: Equipment used to generate radio waves. Most commonly, this radio carrier signal is amplitude varied or frequency varied (modulated) with information and radiated into space.

Transmitter power: The average peak envelope power (output) present at the antenna terminals of the transmitter. The term "transmitted" includes any external radiofrequency power amplifier which may be used.

Ultra High Frequency (UHF): Ultra high frequency radio waves that are in the range of 300 to 3,000 MHz.

Uncontrolled environment: Applies to those persons who have no control over their exposure to RF energy in the environment. Residences adjacent to ham radio installations are considered to be in an "uncontrolled" environment.

Upper Sideband (USB): The proper operating mode for sideband transmissions made in the new Novice 10-meter voice band. Amateurs generally operate USB at 20 meters and higher frequencies; lower sideband (LSB) at 40 meters and lower frequencies.

Very High Frequency (VHF): Very high frequency radio waves that are in the range of 30 to 300 MHz.

Volunteer Examiner: An amateur operator of at least a General Class level who prepares and administers amateur operator license examinations.

Volunteer Examiner Coordinator (VEC): A member of an organization which has entered into an agreement with the FCC to coordinate the efforts of volunteer examiners in preparing and administering examinations for amateur operator licenses.

Index